OUTDOOR MINIMALIST

Waste Less Hiking, Camping, and Backpacking

MEG CARNEY

Illustrations by Savannah Cuthbertson

Essex, Connecticut

An imprint of Globe Pequot, the trade division of
The Rowman & Littlefield Publishing Group, Inc.
4501 Forbes Blvd., Ste. 200
Lanham, MD 20706
www.rowman.com

Falcon and FalconGuides are registered trademarks and Make Adventure Your Story
is a trademark of The Rowman & Littlefield Publishing Group, Inc.

Distributed by NATIONAL BOOK NETWORK

British Library Cataloguing in Publication Information available

Library of Congress Cataloging-in-Publication Data
Names: Carney, Meg, 1992– author.
Title: Outdoor minimalist : waste less hiking, backpacking and camping / Meg Carney ;
    illustrations by Savannah Cuthbertson.
Description: Guilford, Connecticut : Falcon, [2022] | Includes bibliographical references. |
    Summary: "A guide to actionable ways to waste less while hiking and camping and implement
    low-impact practices in outdoor pursuits"— Provided by publisher.
Identifiers: LCCN 2022000002 (print) | LCCN 2022000003 (ebook) | ISBN 9781493063994
    (paperback) | ISBN 9781493064007 (epub)
Subjects: LCSH: Outdoor recreation—Environmental aspects. | Outdoor recreation—Equipment
    and supplies. | Low-impact camping. | Waste minimization.
Classification: LCC GV191.6 .C374 2022 (print) | LCC GV191.6 (ebook) | DDC 796.5—dc23/
    eng/20220125
LC record available at https://lccn.loc.gov/2022000002
LC ebook record available at https://lccn.loc.gov/2022000003

♾️™ The paper used in this publication meets the minimum requirements of American National
Standard for Information Sciences—Permanence of Paper for Printed Library Materials, ANSI/
NISO Z39.48-1992.

FSC
www.fsc.org
MIX
Paper from
responsible sources
FSC® C005010

This book is printed by Forest Stewardship Council© certified printers on FSC© certified paper.

Contents

INTRODUCTION

Wilderness is not a luxury, but a necessity of the human spirit.
—EDWARD ABBEY

TIME SPENT IN THE WILDERNESS IS NOT EASILY QUANTIFIABLE or defined. Ask any avid outdoors person why they spend their hard-earned money and free time finding a remote slice of forest, river, or desert, and their answers will be as vast and varying as the ecosystems that draw them out.

For me, the wilderness brings an immense sense of belonging I have yet to find in other places beyond myself. Belonging in the wilderness may seem like a foreign concept to some, since for many, wilderness is equivalent to the unknown. I personally have an adverse reaction to ambiguity, but for reasons I can't identify, the wild unknown of nature is different. The dry, red earth of the desert and the fragrant forests of the north are places that humans seemingly have no right to roam, let alone claim they own. Despite this, the inseparable feelings of belonging boil down to connectivity and the freedom you have to simply be: to exist with no external pressure beyond meeting your basic human needs and being present in that very moment.

There's likely no need for me to explain the wonders of outdoor experiences to you. If you've picked up this handbook, you probably feel drawn to the wonders of the wilderness, even if you can't articulate it. Writing this book, I only realized the purpose of the text after all but this introduction had been written. The idea when I started was to help convince others to become stewards of the environment within the growing world of outdoor recreation. Now that it is all said and done, I still recognize that to be true, but I realize the true purpose of me sharing this with you is to shorten the learning curve for outdoor activities—to get you more quickly from dreaming to doing.

I've loved being outside since I was a child, but it wasn't until my late twenties that I began to realize how little I knew about the flora and fauna I spent so much of my life traipsing around in. Looking back on a few of my very first solo trips outdoors, I can pick out nearly every mistake I made, from my choice of rain gear (or lack thereof) to how to pack my bag and an unfortunate lack of planning. For many people, starting a new outdoor hobby takes many trials and errors—I know it did for me. Sometimes, we are fortunate enough to be friends with someone with more experience who can shed some light on the vital aspects of that activity, but for others, it is a journey we take alone.

Each year, interest grows in the many sectors of outdoor recreation. As our trails, public lands, and backroads gain more notoriety, a bit of magic in the wild adventure can be lost among the crowds. While that may be a selfish observation, more people means greater impact on the ecosystems where we seek solace. Part of this is due to lack of education or understanding of how to recreate responsibly. Still, when we think of the impact outdoor recreation has on the environment, it is easy to zero in on trail wear, campsite establishment, vandalism, and litter. While all of these things are important and necessary to be aware of and prevent, they are just a few pieces to a much larger puzzle. Books like *No Impact Man*, environmental documentaries, and movements like zero-waste have brought many big-picture problems to light for a much larger audience. Despite this, within the outdoor recreation community, it can sometimes feel like the activities we love have become more of an exploitation of wild spaces than a way to protect them. Some activities can even feel quite elitist, building up a barrier to entry that revolves more around materialistic values than the human experience and our relationship with nature and ourselves.

On a backpacking trip a good friend of mine once said, "it's so alarming that all you really need to live and to be happy, you can carry on your back." In our current consumer culture, it is easy to get caught up in the demands of daily life. We become overwhelmed with the feeling that we need more to be happy. Then, we take a trip out backpacking and realize most of that stuff isn't necessary. We realize most of our daily stresses are somewhat trivial. As outdoor recreation has grown in popularity, though, I've noticed dramatic changes in how we interact with our outdoor spaces. At times, it feels as if we attempt to bring our entire living room outside instead of truly experiencing the nuances and challenges nature presents us. It is as if the simplicity of enjoying time outside is lost among the noise of gadgets, gear, and social media. Anyone who knows me personally can attest that although I will gladly spend days outdoors, I am not a "gearhead." As an outdoor writer, I field questions from friends and family about gear often, and they're surprised when I am not up to date on all the latest gear technologies and instead prefer to analyze purchases through practicality, quality, and longevity, not the brand name or novelty. While I do write some gear reviews and research gear trends for certain writing assignments, to me, there is a fine line between necessity and the "next best" model of outdoor equipment.

My personal growth as an environmentalist stems from the pure enjoyment of being immersed in nature and an evolving appreciation of ecology. It is not a secret that more time spent outside is good for our health, but there is also an idea that the more time you spend outdoors, the more you feel inclined to protect it. We grow into stewards of the earth so that generations beyond us can enjoy the same landscapes we have in our lifetime. Yes, to some, this may seem like a selfish endeavor, and in truth, it is. As humans, we cannot decide the value of a spruce tree, let alone the value of a single blade of grass, but we choose to become a part of their world whether it be positive or negative.

Theoretically, we learn to love where we recreate and do our part to protect it. But then stuff takes over—stuff we buy, stuff we sell, stuff we see in magazines, stuff someone else has that we wish we had, stuff we think we need before we can start. When things take precedence over experience, we begin to fall short on our end of that bargain. Nature continues to offer us beautiful places to explore, but our activities might end up having a net negative impact on those spaces and the future of the planet. The problem with the growth of the outdoor industry has become that the environment continues to suffer instead of being restored and respected. Much of the impact of increased interaction with wild landscapes is negative, intentional or not. It isn't just the outdoor spaces we play in that are damaged, though. In this book, we explore far more than your impact when you are on the trail, but the environmental impact of the outdoor industry as a whole and what you can do about it. This book is for individuals as well as outfitters, tour companies, and gear production companies. It is a reboot of the mindset we have regarding outdoor recreation and how we can implement low-waste and low-impact practices, no matter the activity. The purpose of this book is not to tell you how to do everything right; it is to help you develop and evolve your current mindset surrounding outdoor recreation and your relationship with the environment. From the weekend backpacker to the backyard hammocker and even mountain expeditionists, there's something for everyone to apply to their personal journey.

This book is a combination of firsthand experiences, stories heard from friends and acquaintances, company interviews, and additional research. You can choose to read this book front to back or keep it on hand for a reference to be used while prepping for a trip or when buying new gear. While there is data throughout the text, all chapters include instructions, advice, and various ideas for applying best practices in our outdoor pursuits.

As someone who benefits from spending time in various wild spaces, what started as a selfish journey to save landscapes simply so I can continue to enjoy them has become a lifelong passion for protecting all the life that inhabits the Earth. There is a unique wonder found in wilderness, and it must be shared, but to do that, it must be spared. While the intention of this book is not necessarily to teach you how to backpack or camp, it will give you some of the necessary tools and information you need to approach any form of outdoor recreation through the lens of environmentalism and minimalism. So, as you read on, I hope that you take what you can and apply this information to your life.

No, this book is not the end-all, be-all, perfect way to be low-waste outdoors, but it is an excellent place to start. The concept of outdoor minimalism extends beyond a zero-waste lifestyle while expanding on some of the same ideas. The Zero-Waste International Alliance defines zero-waste as, "the conservation of all resources by means of responsible production, consumption, reuse, and recovery of products, packaging, and materials without burning and with no discharges to land, water, or air that threaten the environment or human health" (EPA, 2021).

Outdoor minimalist practices encourage reducing your impact on the environment while simultaneously strengthening your relationship to nature. The environmentalists' "know, care, do" approach to outdoor recreation includes aspects of zero-waste while expanding them into a minimalist mindset and application to outdoor sports, leisure, and recreation.

Happy reading, and happy trails!

THE LEAVE NO TRACE SEVEN PRINCIPLES

1. Plan Ahead and Prepare

2. Travel and Camp on Durable Surfaces

3. Dispose of Waste Properly

4. Leave What You Find

5. Minimize Campfire Impacts

6. Respect Wildlife

7. Be Considerate of Other Visitors

© Leave No Trace: www.LNT.org

The Seven Rs of
Outdoor Minimalism

Never doubt that a small group of thoughtful, committed citizens can change the world; indeed, it is the only thing that ever has.

—MARGARET MEAD

THE CONCEPT OF MINIMALISM COMES FROM THE ARTS—SIMPLE forms in painting and sculpture; short, repetitive phrases in music. It's about doing more with less: reducing clutter and celebrating simplicity.

Minimalism as an approach to life has come to be known as having less stuff. To some, minimalism will look like being able to fit everything they own into a backpack, while for others, it includes owning a house, a car, and raising a family. Possessions are symptoms, though, not the core of minimalism. More broadly, minimalism is about what is essential. Minimalism brings forth a level of self-awareness of what you truly need in your specific life circumstance, and a realization that your needs are relative within all of life's changes. What is essential is also often associated with a person's ability to be fully present, and in the moment. Consumerism, and even "retail therapy," are ways many of us use to escape our reality, and we use the distraction of excess to hide from our here and now. Minimalism is a journey of self-discovery that bridges necessity with intentionality.

Minimalism, especially outdoor minimalism, should be seen as a way of thinking that influences day-to-day activities, like what we buy. One of the most important aspects of moving toward a lower-impact lifestyle like minimalism is a shift in mindset. We live in a consumer culture of instant gratification that makes us believe more is always better and buying more will make us happy. Minimalism challenges that belief and gradually pushes your mindset from feeling like you should consume more to an evaluation of your needs versus wants. It is the shift from feeling like something external can make you feel fulfilled.

Outdoor pursuits often require paring down. There's nothing like carrying the physical weight of every single item you need to get by for a week in the wilderness to make you think critically about what those needs actually are. If you're reading this, my guess is that you are already looking for ways to reduce your environmental impact and shift your perception of material goods.

Being ready for a change is the first step, but, beyond that, knowing how to actually implement positive changes to all aspects of your life becomes more challenging. Before we dive deep into the specifics of how to implement outdoor minimalism practices into your favorite activities, such as hiking or camping, we need a solid foundation. Cue the seven Rs of outdoor minimalism: reduce, refuse, rethink, repair, rehome (or repurpose), remove, and restore. One of these will be familiar to you because it is the first R in the well-known reduce, reuse, recycle lineup. Unlike these three Rs, the seven Rs of outdoor minimalism go much deeper to challenge the consumer to reflect on a product's whole life cycle and its impact on the environment.

1. REDUCE

Perhaps one of the most essential Rs on either list is "reduce." In terms of outdoor recreation, that means reducing our consumption and reducing our impact on the landscapes we love to explore. Reducing consumption can come in many very impactful forms, such as reducing the amount of plastic packaging we buy, reducing the number of clothing items we buy each year, and reducing how often we replace our outdoor gear.

The reduction of consumption is an important concept, because we live in a consumer-based economy, but we live on a finite planet. Consumer-based societies often treat items and natural resources as infinite, when that is not the case. Reduction of consumption, no matter the area of reduction, then is a way for consumers to take some responsibility and accountability while recognizing that though humans must consume to survive, we have control over what it is we consume and how much of it we consume.

By first implementing the idea that we should be reducing our purchases of consumer goods, we take more control of our finances and begin to gravitate toward purchasing items that will last far longer. Instead of going for the hottest sale item or mindlessly perusing aisle after aisle, what the outdoor minimalist buys gains more purpose and meaning. Yes, we may already be assigning far too much meaning to our material possessions. Still, when restructuring our idea of meaning when it comes to consumer goods, those items no longer as easily define who we are as a person. Material goods simply begin to serve a specific purpose associated with a task in our doing, not in our being.

Reducing our impact comes in many forms. In an outdoor setting, this can look like packing trail snacks in a reusable container, using a reusable water bottle, and packing out what we pack in. In our daily lives, this may mean eating less meat or buying ethically sourced items. Each person will have a different approach to reducing their consumption or impact, and it will evolve with time and exposure to new ideas.

2. Refuse

Some readers may be thinking, "isn't refusing going to be the same thing as reducing?" In some ways, yes, but at its core, it tackles a much deeper concept of minimalism. You see, when we reduce the number of things we are buying, in most circumstances, we are only buying something new (or secondhand) when we can no longer repair or reuse that item. We can *reduce* our impact on the environment, but we can't *refuse* to impact the environment. As long as we are alive, humans will impact the planet and any environment we come into contact with. That's why we work hard to minimize the harm along the way.

When we outright refuse to buy something, it can be seen as a boycott of that specific product. For most of us, this is not going to happen overnight. It takes time to build new habits and to think critically about everything you buy and consume. For instance, when you are buying one item, you can choose to carry the item out in your purse or pocket instead of using a bag. Or before you buy a new pair of running shorts, look through the ones you have and think about how much you *need* a new pair before buying the new ones you liked while scrolling on social media. Refusal is a shift in behavior away from automatic, compulsive purchasing.

By saying no to things like single-use plastics, fast fashion, and animal products, you are telling the producers that you no longer have an interest in supporting their wasteful and exploitative practices. It is a way to "vote with your money."

Many of the environmental issues that we face today are a trickle-down from corporate and government systems, making them feel out of our control. Refusing to consume, when it is appropriate in your life situation, is one of the easiest ways to implement an environmentally positive change into your daily life. You are then effectively shifting from an idea to action.

3. RETHINK

Rethinking is something that you've already begun to do if you are reading this book. Rethinking is one of the seven Rs of outdoor minimalism because it challenges us to reevaluate how we interact with natural spaces, products, waste, and consumption. No one person will be perfect when it comes to reducing or refusing in every aspect of their lives, and for many people, it comes down to accessibility. How much time can you invest in company research or DIYs? What is your financial situation when it comes to investing in quality gear? Are there gear repair shops or outdoor stores in your city? Not everyone will have access to the same knowledge, resources, money, or community support when integrating the reducing and refusing aspects discussed above.

The importance of rethinking is that we no longer see natural resources as infinite or with a sense of ownership. We see products for their entire life cycle and imagine their lasting impacts, acknowledging that natural resources are finite and necessary for life beyond that of humans. We also acknowledge that we've been taught that natural resources are ours to exploit when, in reality, nature is ours to protect and preserve if we want to protect and preserve ourselves. We must begin to acknowledge, if we don't already, that all things are interconnected and we rely on each other to survive.

If you're starting a zero-waste, minimalist, or low-waste journey, the idea of rethinking every purchase or action seems exhausting because it can be. Start with what you know and move out from there. For instance, if you know that an outdoor gear company like Osprey makes backpacks and they offer lifetime repairs, you may want to reconsider that a cheaper alternative will go straight to a landfill if a zipper breaks and you can't fix it. Rethinking purchases and your interaction with outdoor spaces can take more initial research and sometimes means investing more money up front (like buying an Osprey pack vs. an off-brand Amazon pack). In the end, rethinking purchases is one of the easiest ways to cut back on consumption and find products that will last longer.

Rethinking purchases comes down to answering one question: *Is it necessary?* Yes, this is a simple question, but I challenge you, the next time you feel an impulse to buy something, stop, and

The Problem with Landfills

All waste must go somewhere. When consumer and commercial waste is not recycled, reused, incinerated, or disposed of improperly (i.e., littering), then it goes to a landfill. Most landfills are a void in a landscape, often created by quarrying or sometimes as a part of land reclamation. The purpose of a landfill is to reduce waste entering the environment (rivers, oceans, forests, etc.), keep our communities clean, and to prevent the spread of disease by isolating waste to one area.

Since landfills are not only used by individual consumers, but also used by commercial businesses like construction companies, agricultural operations, and more, they quickly can reach capacity. When this happens, the landfill is capped. What this means is that a final layer of organic material is put on top of the landfill waste, the area is reestablished, and can now be used as a recreation area or community grounds of some kind.

While this seems good in theory, and currently landfills are a societal necessity, there are many environmental issues left unresolved. There are a few big problems with the use of landfills:

1. The creation of new landfills requires the destruction of natural habitats with the average landfill size being around 600 acres. As of 2021, there were over 3,000 active landfills and 10,000 closed landfills (Environmental Protection Agency).

2. The production of leachate, a liquid formed when water filters through waste during breakdown. While landfills are required to have a plastic or clay lining, leachate can easily leak through imperfections in the lining. Most leachate contains high levels of ammonia, eventually being nitrified to produce nitrate when it enters an ecosystem. Nitrate can lead to eutrophication (lack of oxygen caused by plant growth) in nearby water sources, creating dead zones.

3. Landfills release greenhouse gases into the atmosphere from decaying waste. The primary greenhouse gas emitted from landfills is methane. Methane is created as organic materials decompose and has eighty times the warming potential of carbon dioxide when it enters the atmosphere (Environmental Defense Fund, 2021).

Although these are the primary environmental issues that landfills present, other secondary issues may include unpleasant views and smells for people that live near the landfill and area gull or rat infestations (Vasarhelyi, 2021).

ask yourself, "is this necessary?" If you even hesitate, don't buy it. Rethink your intention and redirect your attention.

Rethinking your purchasing habits is one thing. Rethinking the implications of what you purchase and every step it takes to get to your door is another. It takes time to get to a spot where you feel confident in every purchase you make. I'm not quite there yet. As I shift my mindset and train my brain to reconsider and reevaluate purchases, I gain a deeper respect and understanding of the process as a whole.

4. REPAIR

Knowing how to repair outdoor gear can not only save you when in the backcountry, but it can save your gear from being "retired" too early. For details on how to repair gear, jump to the "Don't Throw Old Gear Out" chapter of this book. In that chapter, we discuss the importance of learning to repair gear instead of replacing an item anytime even one little part breaks or wears down. When it comes to outdoor gear, many items like backpacks, clothing, tents, and boots use long-lasting materials in the form of polyester or other plastics. Yes, these materials are durable and hold up well outdoors, but that is because plastic never fully biodegrades, and many materials, like nylon, have a high melting point. Both of these aspects make them perfect for rugged out-door use, but impossible to recycle or dispose of in an ecologically responsible way.

Look at the life span of a product like a backpack. It lasts for years but might become effectively useless if one small piece, like a buckle, breaks. Without trying or knowing how to fix the buckle, the whole backpack could be destined for the landfill. The thing is, a simple fix could extend the life of the backpack tenfold. Depending on the brand, the user might not even have to repair it themselves. Yes, they would have to send it to the company and maybe be without a pack for a few weeks, but they also wouldn't have to buy a brand-new pack and would save a lot of plastic from entering the landfill.

5. Rehome/Repurpose

Rehome and repurpose are grouped together because in most cases when you're choosing to rehome or repurpose something, that particular item no longer serves its original purpose. You are ready to move on from using it, and now you need to find some-thing else to do with it. If we take the case of the backpack buckle breaking above, if that person is set on getting a new pack, they also can choose to rehome the pack to someone that maybe can't afford a backpack but is willing to repair the old one.

Then, there comes a time when we simply outgrow a piece of gear, and that's okay. But that doesn't mean that we should throw it in the garbage or just let it degrade in the back of a closet some-where. When you're getting to a point where you need to upgrade your gear, first consider rehoming it. By rehoming something as simple as a decent pair of rain pants, a tent, or a backpack, you likely are giving someone a chance to experience the outdoors when they couldn't afford to do otherwise. It's no secret that high-quality outdoor equipment is expensive, and the high price point makes accessibility to some outdoor experiences feel elitist.

Rehoming gear that is still functional and safe opens up accessibility to others (even if you decide to sell it secondhand).

Repurposing doesn't always work for outdoor equipment, which is part of the reason why it is grouped with rehoming. However, it is possible. For example, an old climbing rope should not be rehomed for safety reasons. To avoid throwing a rope largely made from plastic fibers into the trash, you can donate it to companies, like CragDog, that make dog leashes and toys out of ropes. Or you can invest time into a craft project to make an entry mat from the rope. So, while not every piece of equipment can be repurposed, some of them can, and you'll get more life out of your initial purchase by doing so.

6. REMOVE

The last two Rs have less to do with outdoor equipment and buying habits and more to do with the natural spaces we love to explore. Every time you enter a natural space, be it the neighborhood near your home, a city park, a mountain trail, or the lakes of a wilderness area, you've likely noticed trash left by humans who used the area before you or that was brought by wind or water. No matter how the trash ended up there, it becomes a detriment to your experience, and litter is known to harm plants and animals that call that ecosystem home.

A good practice to get into when using outdoor spaces is to leave it better than you found it. This idea is adopted from a quote by Robert Baden-Powell urging everyone to "try and leave this world a little better than you found it, and when your turn comes to die, you can die happy in feeling that at any rate, you have not wasted your time but have done your best." You may be familiar with this idea if you were in the Boy Scouts growing up, as it has been adopted as the scout's rule.

At its core, leaving a natural space better than you found it means that even if you were not the one who left that beer can or that candy wrapper, you have the shared responsibility to remove it. For some, this may be as simple as bringing an extra bag with you when you are hiking to pick up trash as you go. For others, this may mean getting involved in a local cleanup organization to help remove litter from various areas in your community.

7. RESTORE

The final R of outdoor minimalism is to restore natural areas. Not everyone will have the same ability to effectively restore land in the same way a conservationist or restoration program does. Still, in essence, all outdoor enthusiasts can contribute to land restoration. Within the outdoor community, hunters and anglers are often the most active in habitat restoration. That is partly due to the conservation funds set up to funnel money from hunting and fishing purchases, like licenses and some gear, to conservation organizations. Hunters and anglers also often see a more direct impact of the habitat degradation that their sporting activity has on habitat, making them quicker to take action in an effort to protect the ecosystems but also to protect their personal sporting pursuits.

If you are not involved in hunting or fishing or don't have the funds to donate to conservation programs, the next best thing you can do is donate time, talents, and exposure to your community's conservation efforts. If you have the knowledge and ability to restore small ecosystems like your yard or land, this can be done in partnership with conservation organizations. Many restoration and conservation projects take volunteers for large-scale projects like planting trees or cleaning up an area before restoring.

Another part of restoration is understanding the human impact on the ecosystems you visit or want to restore. If you are backpacking through an area, stay on the trail and get to know how human activity impacts the area. While it can be tempting to go out and plant new trees or flowers, unless you fully understand the ecosystem and the native plants, these attempts should be left to the experts or only done with extensive guidance and research.

All of the seven Rs play an important role in understanding and integrating outdoor minimalism into your life. You can look at all of the Rs except restoration as being preventative measures to protect the outdoor spaces we love. Then, you can consider the last R, restoration, as a way to address the damage that has already been done. Restoration is the hardest of all of the seven Rs of outdoor minimalism to achieve but is perhaps the most important, because it keeps our natural spaces healthy and provides new spaces for generations to come.

As you read and use this book as a resource in your pursuit of outdoor minimalism, use the seven Rs as a foundation and adapt them to your life's situation. As you pursue the practice of minimalism in any aspect of your life, it is important to remember that being imperfect is a part of the process. When first reading the seven Rs, it can be tempting to think that in order to be a true "outdoor minimalist" you must implement all seven at one time, and that you have to do it perfectly. Realize that practices like minimalism and zero-waste are marathons, not sprints.

To approach either one mindfully, it is essential to take things one step at a time and to have an exceptional amount of patience and compassion for yourself along the way. When we are learning and implementing new life practices and habits, it can easily become overwhelming, and having patience during the process affords you more meaningful opportunities for lasting growth and change.

Get to Know Your Gear

No matter the pursuit, any outdoor enthusiast can attest to the importance of quality outdoor equipment. Over time, the quality and quantity of gear available has drastically changed. How do you shop effectively when the options for outdoor equipment are practically endless and new gear is released daily? Faced with overwhelming choices, most of us default to the cheapest option or the brands we know.

As you implement zero-waste or minimalist approaches to your various outdoor activities, one of the best places to start is with your gear. Outdoor gear can be a lot of things. For someone who hikes, it could be their backpack, water bottle, hiking shoes, or sun hat. For someone who kayaks, their gear may include their kayak, paddle, life jacket, sunglasses, or splash skirt. For a climber, it's likely safety equipment like a harness, ropes, cams, stoppers, and slings. Outdoor gear is somewhat unique to the particular outdoor pursuit you are undertaking, but it can essentially be defined as *the physical items that allow you to safely engage in the outdoor activities you enjoy.*

There is some extensive pressure within many sectors of the outdoor industry to have "all the right" or "all the best" gear for every pursuit. Beginners (which we all are at some point) in an outdoor activity often turn to online resources to gather information about the gear and knowledge we need. The internet is an excellent resource for these types of questions, but it can also overwhelm your selection process and what you *deem* as necessary versus what you *actually need* to be successful in that particular activity.

Unfortunately, we don't *actually* need most of the gear that is marketed to us. We are just told that we *should* have it or at least we should want it—it all goes back to the general culture of consumerism. Narrowing down the gear you really need may seem daunting at first, because it is, especially if you are just getting into a new outdoor activity. Needs vary with skill, and outdoor equipment often becomes more about comfort.

To understand this section of the book, let's learn know how to approach outdoor gear with a minimalist mindset in a few easy steps:

1. Evaluate and identify the gear you need to be safe during your outdoor activities.

2. Once you know what you need, start with what you have. If you don't have anything, then ask friends and family if they'd be willing to either lend or give you old gear that is still functional. When that's not an option, choose to buy secondhand equipment or rent gear from an outfitter.

3. Start to understand a product's entire life cycle, not just its life with you, before investing in new gear.

All of these steps help you start on the right path of outdoor minimalist gear selection, but your knowledge of the gear itself is also vital during your selection process.

How Do You Know What Outdoor Gear You *Actually* Need?

Many of us never even learn to identify actual needs. Consumer culture blurs the lines between wants and needs, encouraging us to buy more and more. When applying need vs. want to outdoor minimalism, it can be difficult to know where to start, especially if you are new to an activity.

To identify needs in terms of outdoor recreation, you will need to separate them from your basic human needs of food, shelter, and safety. Once those basic needs are met, then you can branch into secondary needs regarding the types of outdoor gear. Beyond your basic human needs for survival, needs can apply to your requirements for physical and mental wellness. While this can feel like it is blurring the lines between needs and wants, consider that your personal needs can be applied to any type of relationship, including your relationship to self, consumerism, and inanimate objects like gear.

To help guide you through the process of identifying your needs when it comes to outdoor gear, I've chosen four primary areas of consideration:

4. Price

5. Quality

6. Safety

7. Sustainability

There will be overlap between some of these, but dissecting the decision-making process into four distinct areas can help narrow down purchase options as well as dictate the difference between desires and needs.

Price

The first aspect of deciding which gear you need is going to come down to your budget. In a sense, having less money budgeted for outdoor gear and recreational activities is a form of forced minimalism. If you can't always afford the nicest and the newest gear, you are going to invest your money in what you actually need.

After all, you put your energy into earning money, and that money then becomes energy for investing in other life needs.

So the price of an item becomes a driving force in the need or want of an item, especially one you have to save and budget to buy. As an example, before I bought my beloved gravel bike (named Meriwether because I know you needed that information), I knew it was going to be an expensive investment. And I used the word *investment* over purchase, because when the outdoor gear you buy is viewed as an investment versus a purchase, you value it more. A purchase is more closely related to instant gratification, because it is a one-time thing. When you purchase something, you spend your money and then it is gone, whereas an investment is putting your money into something that will yield more results and add value in the long term.

In the grand scheme of life and my basic human needs, did I need a gravel bike? No. I wanted a gravel bike, but I knew that a quality and reliable bike would contribute to my mental, physical, and spiritual happiness—not to mention help cut down motorized travel. In that context, I decided it was a worthwhile investment, and it also falls into the parameters of a personal need as it adds value to my life. With that information, I then decided to pool my energy into making and saving money to invest in a gravel bike. I did not want to rush out to Walmart to buy a bike for a couple hundred dollars. Not only would that cheaper bike likely not last me longer than a year, but I would be putting my money into an unsustainable production model that values profit over resource management and environmental health. I did my research, talked to experienced gravel cyclists, and focused my search on used bikes, allowing me to get a bike of better quality within my price range.

Your budget and the price of items can impact how you perceive personal needs. High-quality gear may be more difficult to find, but that should not diminish the importance of meeting your gear needs. In fact, having to save money to buy outdoor gear can enhance your perceived investment and add more value to your gear in the long run. Price can sometimes dictate the availability of what you can realistically afford, but it does not need to minimize your needs. You just might have to take a different approach.

Quality (and frequency of use)

In a perfect world, we'd always buy the highest-quality gear, no exceptions. That is not a realistic expectation, though, because we do not all have the same resources or even the same interest level in an activity. For instance, I invested heavily in my bike because I love cycling, have for a long time, and know I will continue well into the future. I wouldn't suggest spending $2,000 on a bike for your toddler who'll outgrow it in months or for a casual cycler who bikes a few times a year. Your level of investment in an activity can also impact your level of investment in the quality of equipment.

For many of us, price is going to be and will continue to be the driving force in our purchasing decisions. We also know that we often have to pay more to get a higher-quality item, but if we are willing to pay more, that item will likely last us far longer, making the initial investment worth it in the long run. For the purposes of deciding your needs when it comes to outdoor equipment, quality should be a consideration because you not only want something that works for you but also want it to last through the trials of use.

You might want the very best bike because it's shiny and prestigious, but do you really need it if you only ever bike around your neighborhood? Quality is important, but we need to learn to distinguish between actual value and consumer cachet.

Safety

The next most common consideration when it comes to the need of outdoor equipment is if it improves your level of safety when participating in a particular activity. As mentioned earlier, our experience level in the outdoors and within that activity can drastically change the type and amount of gear necessary for you to be safe in that environment. For instance, I would never tell a first-time backpacker to go ultralight or pursue bushcraft on their own. Those skills take time to cultivate and although you can learn by jumping into the fire, there are far too many deadly situations that could have been prevented by having more knowledge of that environment, your skill level, and the correct equipment.

If a piece of equipment that you use helps you stay safe in the backcountry, I'd qualify that as a need. Even if someone more experienced may not be carrying it or even says it isn't necessary, they are not you, and they do not have the same knowledge base as you. It is imperative to not compare yourself to others when engaging in outdoor recreational activities, because more often than not, you will get yourself into a situation that you are not prepared to handle.

So, when deciding if you need a piece of equipment, first consider if it increases your level of safety. Comfort is a secondary concern.

Sustainability

As you analyze your needs when it comes to outdoor gear, sustainability should become a part of the larger picture. The quality of your gear is often reflected by the materials they are made out of, and those materials in many instances are not sustainable or environmentally friendly. We are starting to see a shift, especially in the outdoor industry, as companies make more of an effort to produce sustainable products, but with certain industry and consumer standards it is difficult to always meet those expectations.

So, unfortunately, when you are looking at your needs when it comes to gear, sustainability is often put last when it should be first. However, sustainability does not always need to be associated with environmental impact. For gear purposes, sustainability can also mean how sustainable it is for you to continue to use that item for its intended use. This can then tie back to frequency of use. Back to the bike example: If cycling does not fit your lifestyle and you wouldn't consistently use a bike, it would not be a sustainable purchase. The word sustainable is defined as, "able to maintain at a certain rate or level." With that definition in mind, consider whether or not you can sustain a lifestyle that utilizes gear effectively before making a purchase. If you can't, then you probably don't need it.

There are times when you may not know if you are going to like an activity or not yet, but you want to try it out. In those instances, you may not know how often you will ultimately engage in that activity. In this scenario, the best approach would be to rent or borrow equipment so you can try the activity for a short time. Then, if you enjoy it, you can invest in gear appropriate for you.

WHAT TO DO ONCE YOU'VE IDENTIFIED YOUR GEAR NEEDS

Identifying the gear you need and will in fact use regularly is only one part of the selection process. As you are narrowing down the list of gear you want to invest in, also take inventory of what you already own and use. Once you've done that, begin the process of shopping for new or used gear.

When you are acquiring outdoor gear, especially if you are new to an activity like backpacking, I will always recommend trying to get your gear secondhand. Secondhand gear is less expensive for the consumer, prevents further resource extraction to produce a new product, and it also helps redirect goods from the landfill. Be mindful that not all outdoor equipment is safe to get secondhand, though. For instance, climbing equipment designed for safety should be purchased new in almost all circumstances, so you know it has gone through product testing and has not been tampered with or damaged. For other outdoor gear, like clothes, packs, and tents, you can find decent and functional used products.

Buying secondhand when adopting outdoor minimalist practices helps divert equipment from landfills and remove unnecessary waste in the form of consumer demand. Buying secondhand doesn't just have to look like sifting through racks at a thrift store either. With technology being part of our daily lives, various platforms provide secure transactions and easy shopping. Large outdoor retailers, like REI, also sell used and returned equipment at marked-down prices, or you can find local shops like the Great Lakes Gear Exchange in Duluth, Minnesota, that sell high-quality used gear.

On the flip side, maybe you have *too much* outdoor equipment but still want to take a fresh, new approach and integrate a minimalist mindset. In this case, again, start with what you have. Instead of looking into where to get new gear, focus on what pieces of gear you actually use and need. Then, start downsizing. This process is similar to decluttering in any other part of your life, like your closet. Once you minimize the sheer volume, it becomes easier to zoom in on your gear's most important aspects, like quality and frequency of use.

Even those who seemingly have all the gear they could ever need end up buying new gear from time to time. While I will almost always encourage you to buy secondhand, I know it isn't always accessible or ideal. For many outdoor enthusiasts, buying new gear takes time and research, not to mention budgeting. When you start to consider the entire life cycle of a product, every purchase holds more weight. That means considering all of the resources needed from material extraction through production, transportation, packaging, longevity, and afterlife (landfill, recycle, compost, etc.).

So, when buying new gear, it may take a little extra effort on your part to learn about the company you are buying from. Identifying sustainable companies and high-quality brands starts with transparency. As consumers, we often only see the product life in terms of in-use and then when we need to get rid of the item. The reality is that all of our outdoor gear is made from plant and animal sources or fossil fuels that are extracted from the Earth, produced to make a useful product, and then transported for sale. As consumers, we then use the product until it wears out and needs replacing, and then dispose of it in some way. When getting rid of a product, there is an "out of sight, out of mind" attitude toward many goods, but we also need to consider the product's afterlife. All of these stages of a product's life impact the environment, so they should be considered while shopping.

Yes, your gear's functionality should also be in question, and sometimes you can't get around choosing functionality over sustainability. However, when afforded the opportunity, especially when buying items like clothing or backpacks where safety is not their core value, looking into company practices will tell you how sustainable their products are.

By far, one of the biggest hurdles that many consumers will face when looking to buy sustainable outdoor gear is the price. Many of the most environmentally friendly brands are smaller companies that are passionate about environmentalism and producing a quality product with best practices. That means that they aren't cutting corners to save money and make a profit. They're in it to solve a problem. If they're unwilling to budge on material sourcing, location of manufacturing, paying fair wages, and many other aspects of sustainability, then their product is likely to be more expensive than alternatives.

Many consumers shop solely based on the price of an item. Even durability isn't being considered. It takes time, effort, and a good knowledge base of legitimate, sustainable practices to shop with environmental sustainability and ethical practices in mind. This consumer mindset is a huge hurdle for small businesses that refuse to engage in unethical practices and strive to continually be better because they know when they're making their product right, it isn't going to be the most affordable or most accessible to lower-income consumers.

So, how can consumers gain more awareness of sustainable practices and identify them when shopping for new gear?

There is a laundry list of nuances when it comes to identifying a sustainable product of any kind. The first place to look is company messaging and general marketing strategies. Research the company online ahead of time, even if you'll eventually make your purchase in-store.

Outdoor brands tend to lead their marketing campaigns and branding with sustainability features because they are proud

Signs of a Sustainable Outdoor Product

- Read the company mission statement. Does it align with ethical and environmentally friendly viewpoints?
- Read the company About Us page. Did they start their company to help solve a problem beyond making a functional product? If so, is it to provide a more sustainable option for consumers?
- See if they have a blog or resources page on their website. Are they sharing detailed information about how the product is made, where their materials are coming from, how to repair items, etc.?
- They offer reports and annual reviews outlining targets and goals for sustainable sourcing, energy use, and environmental impact.
- Direct and transparent consumer messaging, including responsiveness to consumer questions regarding sustainability.
- Look for external (third-party) certifications that hold them to a regulated higher standard of environmental stewardship.
- They have a sustainability consultant or advisor to audit environmental and workplace sustainability.
- They have a repair policy and lifetime guarantee for all gear and equipment.
- When the media or consumers call them out regarding production practices, they make a noticeable effort to change and improve beyond a public apology.

supporters of their environmental initiatives. However, be wary of this "image" because, in some cases, that's all it is. Companies with true production transparency make it easy to find information regarding the materials they use, sourcing, production standards, and more. After all, if they genuinely use ethical and sustainable practices, why wouldn't they be proud of sharing it with their customers?

Even with all of these signs of a sustainable product, we can easily become overwhelmed with "green" marketing campaigns. Within the broad range of "green" marketing, beware of greenwashing. Greenwashing is essentially a marketing technique used to convince consumers that a product is more eco-friendly than it is. Greenwashing is often carried out in the form of product messaging, marketing claims, and packaging appearances.

Take compostable or biodegradable plastic, for example. Plastic can break down, but it is not technically a biodegradable

How to Recognize Greenwashing in an Outdoor Company

- There is no proof of their claims.
- Environmental messaging is extremely vague (i.e., all-natural, eco-friendly).
- Product messaging is focused solely on one environmental issue.
- They are not using legitimate third-party certifications to support their initiatives.
- Marketing boasts a "lesser of two evils" type message.
- Lack of transparency in sourcing, production, and transportation as well as general company environmental standards.
- Nonresponsiveness to consumer inquiries regarding environmental practices.

material (Chamas et al., 2020). The plastic pieces simply become smaller and smaller microplastics over time. Some of these materials can, in a sense, be composted, but only in industrial facilities that can provide specific environmental conditions. You cannot compost plastic materials in your at-home compost. That's why getting to know the materials and afterlife of a product is so important. Not all terms like *biodegradable* or *compostable* are regulated in a way that makes it easy for the consumer to understand the afterlife impact.

When trying to avoid the greenwashing of products, it is a good idea to familiarize yourself with some trustworthy certifications. One certification to always look for in outdoor gear is the Certified B Corp. According to the Certified B Corporation website, "The B Corp community works toward reduced inequality, lower levels of poverty, a healthier environment, stronger communities, and the creation of more high-quality jobs with dignity and purpose. By harnessing the power of business, B Corps use profits and growth as a means to a greater end: positive impact for their employees, communities, and the environment." This lofty language is backed up by a rigorous certification process that is renewed regularly with a material commitment to giving back.

There are other certifications like 1% for the Planet and Climate Neutral that may draw your attention. These are amazing programs that encourage companies to support environmental stewardship and take their carbon footprint into account. However, they do not directly correlate to production practices. Take 1% for the Planet as an example. What this means is that companies are donating 1 percent of their annual sales to environmental organizations, usually of their choice. Then, you have carbon offsets that allow for carbon neutrality to exist. In a similar vein, being carbon neutral can mean paying out a sum of money to "offset" or counter the emissions the production of that product is putting out into the environment. These are not necessarily signifiers of sustainable production practices, but they do demonstrate that a company is trying to take positive action. So, do not ignore these positive aspects of a company, but take it with a grain of salt and acknowledge that it doesn't necessarily reflect their production practices. It simply demonstrates that they're aware they have an impact and are working to fulfill the last R of outdoor minimalism, restoration.

Some companies have good intentions when it comes to environmental practices, but let's be honest, not all business owners know "best" environmental practices. For many businesses, it takes some trial and error, and for others, the sheer cost of using more sustainable practices outweighs the perceived benefits of a lower-impact option. With different values and cost investments, although a company may have the ability to use more environmentally friendly practices, they still might be focusing on profit. In this case, the consumer can help apply pressure to effect a positive change. This can be as simple as an email inquiry about more product transparency, or gathering forces with friends, family, or social media followers to push for more of an investment in things like fair wages, nonplastic packaging, or better repair policies.

Even brands that strive for sustainability benefit from consumer questions and comments. Your questions may seem simple, but sometimes it is something that they've never thought of before and can use to better serve the consumer and the health of the planet.

Small, local companies focused on consumer satisfaction are especially responsive to consumer questions. As companies grow, it becomes more difficult to keep up with consumer inquiries, but most of the time, companies working with the planet's and consumer's best interests in mind will make time to make your voice heard. After all, consumers are what keep them in business. If you reach out with questions about specific concerns or practices and continue to receive no response, you can assume that they do not want to talk about that aspect of their production or product manufacturing because it does not meet certain environmental standards.

[See the end of the chapter for email scripts.]

Identifying Sustainable Product Materials

If you feel like you have narrowed down a few trustworthy companies and they seem very transparent with their environmental claims, here comes the hard work: knowing which product materials are sustainable.

There is no getting around the fact that as a society, we rely heavily on materials like plastic, despite their environmental impacts. We use plastic in outdoor gear for packaging, component parts, materials like polyester, and much more. So, as consumers, if we are faced with an ocean of plastic and no better option, what can we do?

First things first: you're already on the right path by reading this book because you are taking the time to educate yourself about how to take action. Second, there may be some alternatives, and if there aren't, learn how to take care of those products so they do not go to waste.

As consumers, we must acknowledge that all products that we use come from somewhere. We often talk about sourcing when discussing where our food is grown, but the same conversation needs to happen when it comes to our outdoor gear and clothing. Where commonly used materials like cotton or hemp are grown, how they're grown, and where they are milled are equally as important as the packaging they come in, their durability, and their afterlife. Or what materials like polyester or Gore-Tex are made of, how they're made, and their whole life cycle impact.

When looking at clothing and textiles specifically, cotton and hemp are often touted as a "saving grace" of sorts for sustainable fabrics. However, as outdoor enthusiasts, you know the many downfalls that fabrics like cotton have. There is even an adage warning against wearing cotton: "cotton kills." This saying comes

Common Materials Used in Outdoor Gear That Are Unsustainable

- **Polyester:** a petroleum-based fiber making it a carbon-intensive nonrenewable resource.

- **Recycled Polyester (rPET):** When recycled from other polyester clothing, rPET has some pros, but all plastics have a finite recyclability. It will still release microplastics, but it releases less carbon than virgin polyester. Some companies turn plastic bottles into rPET fabrics, but beware, some of these companies are also the producers of the plastic bottles they recycle into fabrics.

- **Acrylic Fabric:** made using polymer fibers created from fossil fuels making it a carbon-intensive nonrenewable resource.

- **Conventional Cotton:** involves extensive use of pesticides and fertilization during growing, along with high water usage to grow and to manufacture into clothing.

- **Nylon:** a synthetic material made from petrochemicals that is very energy intensive to produce and is not biodegradable.

- **Rayon Viscose:** made from plants, like bamboo or trees, but is considered semisynthetic because of the highly chemical mechanical process to make the cellulosic fibers. It is not produced in the United States due to the toxic nature of production not fitting within EPA guidelines. Sourcing often comes from monoculture forest productions that destroy natural ecosystems.

- **Some Wool:** limited animal welfare enforcement to protect against animal abuse and no standardized method of wool production within farming practices. Land and

(continued)

Common Materials Used in Outdoor Gear That Are Unsustainable (*continued*)

resources are used to farm sheep for wool production, and extensive water use for wool production from feeding the sheep to producing wool products.

- **Down:** While many reports represent down as the most environmentally friendly insulator, the use of live animal production in terms of resources along with the prolific and inhumane practice of live animal plucking makes it difficult for down to be labeled strictly as a sustainable material.

- **Leather:** Raising cows contributes to deforestation, eutrophication, methane release, and extensive water and fossil fuel usage. Then the process of turning their skin into leather in the United States involves chrome-tanning, which requires the use of chemicals all considered hazardous by the United States EPA.

- **Fabric Blends:** Natural materials like merino wool and hemp are often blended with synthetics like nylon or spandex to improve performance and durability. When blended with a synthetic, it makes the natural material unable to be composted and it makes the synthetic unable to be recycled.

- **PVC (Polyvinyl Chloride):** Commonly known as vinyl, PVC has earned its reputation as potentially the most environmentally damaging plastic through production, use, and disposal. It releases toxic, chlorine-based chemicals that build up into the water, air, and enter the food chain.

- **Gore-Tex:** made from the highly toxic group of chemicals called perfluorochemicals (PFCs) which are also used to make Teflon and contaminate the air, water, and our bloodstreams.

- **Many solvents and glues:** often made from toxic chemicals and becomes a pollutant due to improper disposal.

More Sustainable Materials to Look For in Outdoor Gear

- **Tencel:** similar material to rayon but uses a circular, closed-loop production process that does not produce effluents (heavily contaminated pollutants). It is made from wood by creating a pulp and a drying process called spinning.

- **Hemp:** one of the most sustainable plants that can be used for textiles as it can be farmed intensively, produces more pulp per acre than wood, is biodegradable, and has regenerative properties like returning nutrients to the soil and sequestering carbon dioxide. Hemp fabrics are made by taking long strands of fiber found in the stalk of the plant and separating them from the bark in a process called retting. They can then be spun together to produce a continuous thread to be woven into fabric.

- **Bamboo:** can be sustainable pending the production process and the use of chemicals as it can follow a similar production process to that of rayon. Bamboo as a plant is very sustainable as it grows quickly, requires little water or fertilizer, and can sequester large amounts of carbon dioxide. The process in which bamboo textiles are made decides if that material is environmentally friendly or not.

- **Organic Linen (Flax):** One of the oldest and widely used fabrics in the world, linen is a functional, sustainable, and ethical material. Organic linen is made from the flax plant. All parts of the flax plant are used to make linen, leaving no waste behind, and flax is a recyclable

(continued)

Common Materials Used in Outdoor Gear That Are Unsustainable (*continued*)

fiber. It requires almost no chemical treatment to produce and no irrigation to be grown.

- **Some Wool and Alpaca:** The Responsible Wool Standard (RWS) helps to make wool production more sustainable, but there are still some ethical issues in production globally. Other certifications like Certified Organic Wool and Certified Animal Welfare Approved exist, but RWS tends to have more reliable enforcement. Wool is an animal-based fiber, making it very strong, natural, and biodegradable. Alpaca can be a comparable fabric to wool. Only one company currently manufactures alpaca textiles suitable for outdoor recreation, the Appalachian Gear Company. They use ethical sourcing, take a holistic sustainability approach, and manufacture in the United States.

- **Recycled Steel and Aluminum:** Both can be recycled indefinitely, so ensure the product materials can continue to be recycled when the product reaches end of life with you.

from the fact that cotton is not moisture-wicking, and when it gets wet from rain or sweat, it takes a long time to dry, which is potentially dangerous in certain environments. Waxed cotton does exist, and it is waterproof, but it is really heavy. Hemp is a wonderfully sustainable plant that can be used to make fabrics. Still, very few companies use it, because they prefer softer fabrics or because of the limited options when it comes to hemp cultivation and mills in the United States.

Not to mention that no matter how you spin it, any type of fabric is going to have exceptionally high water and energy usage, it may come from unethical labor practices in both factory and farm settings, the plants used to make the materials likely used dangerous herbicides and pesticides—and there are many other potential environmental dilemmas (Ellen MacArthur Foundation, 2020). Some materials will be more detrimental than others, but avoiding any of these harmful aspects along the supply chain takes extensive research and awareness for a company to succeed. Well, if that's all true, then what are consumers to do? Are nonorganic hemp or cotton shirts more sustainable than polyester or plastic-based alternatives or does the switch make a difference at all?

Yes, plastics are a detriment to the planet. Still, many outdoor enthusiasts gravitate toward polyester clothing and use plastic-based or synthetic fabrics for backpacks, tents, and more. Polyester (and other plastic-based fabrics) are all made using fossil fuels. As most environmentalists agree, fossil fuels are less than ideal when it comes to production. Plastics also do not biodegrade, polyester fabrics are not continuously recyclable, and they shed dangerous microplastics into the environment. So, why are we still choosing these fabrics and hailing them as the best option for outdoor activities if they have a negative impact every step of the product life cycle?

The simple answer is performance and protection. When we are doing anything outdoors, we want to be comfortable and safe. So, there seems to be no getting around the fact that polyester and other synthetic fabrics are seen to be more durable and effective, especially in an outdoor setting. One of the reasons why they work better is also one of the environmental cons: They do not biodegrade. Durability is an asset in outdoor gear, *and* it means synthetic materials never fully decompose. Materials like nylon tend to have a very high melting point, and synthetic fabrics do not absorb or hold water. Again, great for outdoor use, bad for disposal. Natural fibers will decompose naturally, making them less durable in the long run. The good news is that more of an effort is being put into working with natural fibers in the outdoor industry to develop materials and natural fabric blends that are durable and perform well.

Despite these roadblocks, we can continue to evaluate the impact of commonly used materials within the outdoor industry to make more informed decisions about what we are buying. While we are doing this, it is easy to get stuck on one aspect of a product when we need to be looking at the bigger picture. If a company is genuinely transparent, you will know where the product is made, the materials used, where those materials were sourced from, and the impact those materials have. As consumers, we should expect a company to give us a longevity projection for durability, life span, and product afterlife as well.

We often focus on clothing when talking about textiles like shirts and pants, but think about all of the other outdoor gear you own that involves a fabric of some kind. Bags use a lot of fabric, and then you have tents, sleeping bags, bivouac sacks, sleeping pads, shoes, the seats of your car, etc. The list could go on, but we often fixate on clothing because of fast fashion when in fact, the textile industry extends far beyond pants, shirts, and jackets. We also need to remember that the base material is not the only part of the item contributing to an environmental impact. Yes, the base material plays a huge role in that material's environmental impact, but other things like dyes, coatings, and production pollution in the forms of wastewater management and greenhouse gas emissions need to be considered. Textiles in general, no matter the application in fashion or outdoor gear, use nearly 800 billion gallons of water each year. Not only that, but the practice of dyeing and treating textiles accounts for 20 percent of industrial water pollution (Ellen MacArthur Foundation, 2020).

With so many different textiles to consider when shopping for gear, it is easy to pay more attention to the "big ticket" items versus the small, less expensive ones like food bags, stuff sacks, and even the towel we choose. Towels are one of the most versatile items you can have on a packing list, and they are often overlooked. Most backpackers choose lightweight microfiber towels as an option for reasons similar to why we'd choose moisture-wicking fabrics for our clothing and plastic-based fabrics for our tents. While we may not be able to get away from plastic-based materials in all of our outdoor textiles, we should avoid them when we can!

When looking for the perfect backpacking towel, beyond avoiding petroleum-based fabrics, you need to consider durability, absorption, how fast it dries, and if it is sanitary (antimicrobial). Flax linen, one of the more-sustainable fabrics listed above, is a great option for towels. Lava Linens is one brand behind quality backpacking towels made from flax, with transparent sustainability information published on their website and central to their mission. Beyond having a fantastic product, what I love about Lava Linens is that their purpose goes far beyond selling a quality towel. They aim to educate and challenge consumers to stop and think differently when it comes to consumerism. It can be challenging for any company to dig deep when it comes to product marketing because consumers crave short, instant messaging, but that mindset is exactly what the concept of outdoor minimalism is here to challenge. When it comes to the environmental impact of a product, short and sweet messaging isn't always reliable and often leads to greenwashing. Product transparency like Lava Linens demonstrates challenges consumers to think critically about purchases but also gives consumers an expectation to hold other brands accountable.

Textile manufacturing is vast and complex with no perfect solution for completely sustainable production of durable goods. Here's the main thing to remember: No matter what the material is, it has an impact. When looking at all possible materials, it is easy to see how it can become overwhelming to choose which is the best option for your needs. That's why the entire process is important to factor into the equation, only once your needs have been decided.

While textiles play a huge role in the outdoor industry and outdoor gear, fabrics are not the only consideration we need to have when choosing outdoor gear. Right now, the majority of our industrial or consumer systems and companies are considered to be linear production models, not circular systems. Within a linear model, we are taking more resources than we can give back to feed consumer demand for cheap, easy, and instant products.

A circular system can often be confused with a reuse system, which is what many consumers associate with the act of recycling a product. Within the reuse system, we follow the same steps we do in a linear production model, but in between consumption and disposal, we add recycling. When we recycle an item, those materials can then (in some cases) jump back to the production phase and gain a new life. This is a great model *in theory*, because it allows us to continue with the current production model with minimal changes while also diverting materials from the landfill.

Five Steps of Linear Production Model

1. **Extraction:** Raw materials are taken from the earth. Most are nonrenewable, like fossil fuels. Others, like cotton, are technically renewable resources but irresponsible production practices deplete soil health and water supply.

2. **Production:** Extracted materials are processed into finished goods. Production requires energy and additional resources and harms communities through pollution and exploitative labor.

3. **Distribution:** Finished goods are packaged and shipped from factories to warehouses and eventually point of sale via air, sea, trucks, or trains.

4. **Consumption:** This stage of the product's life where it is with the consumer, being used.

5. **Disposal:** Consumer tosses items in the trash or recycling bin. Once we have tossed the item in the designated bin, it is no longer seen as our responsibility.

The problem with the reuse model is that we don't actually know what is happening once an item is recycled, or even if what we put in our recycling bin is in fact recycled. The reality of recycling is that a very small percentage (9 percent) of items put into recycling bins are recycled (American Chemistry Council, 2017). Second, materials, like plastic, can only be recycled a certain number of times. Many materials go through the process of downcycling in order to make recycling plausible. For example, plastic bottles are often downcycled to become plastic bags or other single-use plastic items. In short, this type of recycling does give new life to items, but only for a short time, and those materials eventually end up in landfills. We should only consider true recycling to be when all of the materials are used to produce something of equal, not lesser, value. The reality is that through each recycling process, the plastic bottles' value goes down and it becomes a flimsier object each time. The concept of downcycling does not necessarily apply when a material can be recycled indefinitely (i.e., steel or glass).

That brings us to a circular system or circular economy. Recycling plays a role in circularity, but it can't be the backbone. That would be a reuse system as mentioned above. A circular production model is most comparable with a zero-waste system, and often seen in gardening or market farming. In a circular model, the basic flow starts the same as a linear one, but it does not end. The flow of the system can be simplified to be extraction, production, distribution, consumption, reuse, repurpose, return, and repeat. Within a circular model, there is no need for the disposal aspect of production because everything is either reused, repurposed, or returned. The return aspect of a circular model is essential because it acknowledges that the Earth's resources are finite and must be replenished, not exploited.

Let's look at linear versus circular production through the lens of two widely popular low-waste food storage solutions: the Stasher bag and the Khala & CO reusable food wraps.

Both of these companies have set out to solve the same problem: lessen the amount of packaging waste we create by replacing single-use plastic bags and plastic wrap with a reusable option. This is a wonderful concept and has caught on in the zero-waste movement quickly, and in the world of outdoor recreation because much of what we eat in the backcountry comes in single-use packaging. It is not my intention to say which company came up with the better solution, but we can use this comparison to highlight a decision a consumer may have to make when deciding which food packaging to take on their next backpacking trek. For this example, we will be looking primarily at production choices, the materials used, and afterlife.

Let's look at Stasher bags first (there are many off-brands of this product, but Stasher is the primary company for reusable silicone bags). Stasher bags are made out of food-safe silicone. From the information provided on their website, they are transparent and answer many consumer questions surrounding sustainability. For instance, they state that Stasher bags are designed in California but are produced responsibly in China. This statement seems somewhat vague on its own, but they also clarify that they are a Certified B Corp. Being a Certified B Corp means that they maintain responsible practices and high ethical and environmental standards. These practices are upheld by third-party visits to factories, and the certification ensure they maintain open communication with suppliers. These are good transparent values to communicate to the consumer.

But what exactly is silicone, and why is it better than plastic? Silicone is a material that is made from a combination of silicon (a crystalline solid) and oxygen. It is more durable than plastic and it can be utilized as a gel, when in a rubbery texture like Stasher bags, or when it is hard. Unlike plastics that are made from extracting crude oil from the ground, silicone is made by heating silica with carbon to extract the silicon. Then, a polymer is created by passing the silicon through hydrocarbons. These hydrocarbons that are used to make silicone, however, originate from nonrenewable sources like natural gas or oil, making silicone a nonbiodegradable material.

That leads us to another question Stasher answers: What is the afterlife of their silicone bags? Unfortunately, silicone is not easily recyclable, and as we know from its production, it is not biodegradable. To get around these roadblocks, Stasher participates in the Terracycle program to repurpose Stasher bags that no longer are usable. They also encourage consumers to continue to use them for things other than food if possible. Their repurposing program does divert the silicone from landfills, but it doesn't necessarily create a circular system.

As mentioned, Stasher does repurpose their silicone, but this only moves their product into the reuse production model, which is still a step up from the linear model. Stasher makes it easy to use their repurpose program. Once they receive unusable Stasher bags, their partnership with Terracycle turns that silicone into something new like playground or track surfaces. This is a very innovative program, but it doesn't necessarily eliminate the waste within the afterlife of the silicone material. At some point, silicone will be replaced and likely cannot be recycled, therefore diverting it to a landfill as its end of life or afterlife.

Now, let's take a look at Khala & CO reusable food wraps. These are a very similar concept to that of Stasher bags, and they both have positives and negatives when it comes to their functionality. A positive is that both companies are exceedingly transparent with their customers and are looking to eliminate unnecessary plastic waste.

Khala & CO produce their reusable food wrap with a blended organic hemp and cotton fabric coated with either beeswax or candelilla wax. They chose to do a blend of hemp and cotton because when hemp is used as a stand-alone fabric it is quite stiff and rough, so mixing it with cotton makes it easier to use. They make and package the wraps in Colorado but source fabric and wax elsewhere. Seeing this is all positive, but it should then make you wonder, where is the hemp and cotton being grown? Where is it being milled? Is wax sustainable?

They do their best to source within the United States when possible and consider the entire process when making decisions. They source organically grown hemp and cotton within the United States, as well as beeswax. Since taking beeswax from bees is another form of extraction (that's also not vegan-friendly), they also have candelilla wax. The traditional way of harvesting candelilla wax uses a dangerous sulfuric acid process, creating unsafe working conditions. To avoid worker exploitation, they found a company that uses citric acid from fruits and pays their workers a living wage. Although there is one hemp mill in the United States, they choose to mill the hemp outside the country because they have more ethical and sustainable practices, which outweighs the negatives of sourcing outside of the country. As you can tell, there is a lot of dedication, research, and compromise that has gone into creating a product that works well and minimizes the human footprint.

Beeswax Isn't Vegan?

Beeswax is considered to be a natural, and renewable resource. However, it isn't vegan. Why?

Beeswax is obtained from melting the bee's honeycomb using boiling water and then straining and cooling it into a wax. That process in itself does not harm the bees, but within the moral view of veganism it is an exploitation of bees, and vegans do not believe in using animal products of any kind, no matter the application.

Beeswax is often seen as a sustainable and environmentally friendly resource because it can be harvested from the bees without causing them harm during the harvesting period. Bees make it themselves, and there is limited processing involved making it more sustainable. Regardless, beeswax is an animal byproduct and therefore is not considered vegan.

In consideration of the whole product life, Khala & CO put a lot of focus on the afterlife of their product. Their wraps are entirely biodegradable and compostable because they are made of natural fibers. There is a bit of a catch to their product being truly compostable, though. It only lasts so long, and depending on how often you use it, it may only be usable for 1–2 years. The wax coating does protect the fabric, but as the wax breaks down and disappears, the cloth is then compromised and also begins to break down.

As you can see, there are pros and cons to both products. Anytime you are comparing two items on your gear list, it can be helpful to do a deep dive into materials, production, and afterlife like I did above and make a pros and cons list before you make a final decision.

Khala & CO is a unique example because they are one of the most environmentally driven and transparent companies within the zero-waste market. They are growing fast, but they strive to continue to improve their practices and flaunt transparency to the consumer. That's not to say that Stasher isn't doing great things. In the end, the decision is up to the consumer, but sometimes you

Stasher

- **Pros:** reusable, can be repurposed, certified B-Corp, transparent with customers, easy to use and wash
- **Cons:** falls within the reuse production model, can't repair if it rips, silicone materials, produced in China

Khala & CO

- **Pros:** reusable, biodegradable materials, ethically sourced and produced, transparent with customers, easy to use, has a thought-out afterlife
- **Cons:** only lasts 1–2 years of use, not fully waterproof

have to take a deep dive into company practices and consider your unique values and needs to select the right product.

When trying to buy a new product that fits a specific need, such as food packaging in our example above, it is easiest to narrow it down to a few companies you think may be quality options. Then, you can dive into their product's whole life cycle from there. Yes, this takes some extra time and effort, but once you find a transparent and reliable product, you will likely stick with that company for life because they have instilled trust and been transparent from the start.

LET'S TALK PRODUCT PACKAGING

There is a lot to say about packaging, and I will not say it all here. Much of this topic overlaps with food packaging so when it comes to nitty gritty details of how to properly dispose of certain materials, please go to the "Rethink Trail Food" chapter of the book.

To avoid too much repetition, in this section, I will detail common types of packaging used in the outdoor industry to protect, ship, and sell outdoor clothing and gear, as well as which ones you should try to gravitate toward when buying any item.

It's nearly impossible to know how much packaging waste is generated in shipping, but scores of plastic, pallets, and boxes hold and protect products in transportation and are disposed of behind the scenes. The consumer can only really know the packaging that is on the product when they receive it. Packaging is also a marketing tool. Especially in stores, a company can use design and language to appear more environmentally friendly than they are—a great example of greenwashing. Companies will often use natural color schemes and vague language to appear green. That's what makes deciding to buy a new product for the first time in the store difficult, because you do not have full access to the company website or the time to look it all up at that moment.

Before we jump right into the packaging portion of this section, let's look at some of the pros and cons of shopping in person

Shopping in Person

- **Pros:** try and test products in person, customer assistance for most outdoor stores, easier returns, you can refuse a bag, and some items come in less packaging at the store
- **Cons:** it takes more time and is generally less convenient, limited variety of goods, and you have to commute to the location (possibly multiple locations)

Shopping Online

- **Pros:** easier to compare and contrast multiple items, ability to deeply research the company, product reviews from verified customers, more of a guarantee the item is in stock, easier to buy in bulk, and you can do it from home
- **Cons:** higher chance of fraud, return fees, you can't try or test items, shipping fees, you have to wait to receive your item at least 2 days, and the possibility of more packaging

versus online. For most of us, online shopping has become our go-to or at the very least, a way to research and compare items before going to the store.

One method isn't greener than the other. If we are talking strictly about greenhouse gas emissions, if you live in a city, ordering online can be better unless you walk, bike, or use public transportation to get to the store. If you bundle your orders or buy in bulk online though, this can be just as effective because it not only cuts down on packaging but it is often coming directly from the warehouse. Some online retailers offer an option for "green shipping" or "naked packaging" for certain products. For those who don't live in a city, you may need to rely on online shopping to get certain products. It comes down to very specific details as far as which option is the "greener" solution for your life, as well as accessibility in budget, transportation, and location.

Within much of the zero-waste movement, I see an enormous focus put onto packaging, especially plastics. This is not a *bad* thing, but in the grand scheme of things, putting *all* of your effort and energy into diverting single-use plastics or product packaging in general from the landfill has less of an impact than other efforts like reducing consumption and having targeted, intentional consumption. To be frank, hyperfocusing on avoiding all or even specific packaging is going to leave you exhausted quickly. Instead of fixating on the packaging, focus more on the product itself. Here is where it overlaps—reduction of waste and mindful consumption leads to reduction of packaging waste. It is a win-win scenario when you start with being mindful as it leads you to reducing the amount of packaging waste in your life.

Even with that mindset, there will be waste from packaging. So, once you get to a point when you feel comfortable with your intentional minimization of consumption, then begin to shift your view to include the product packaging as well. I put it in this order because sometimes you may be choosing between two products, but one product is more sustainably produced than the other. The only thing is, the product that is more sustainably made comes in a recycled single-use plastic package destined for the landfill when the other product option utilizes a compostable bamboo package. That right there is greenwashing, whether it be intentional or not. It is cheaper for most companies to invest in sustainable packaging versus sustainable production for the entire life cycle of a product. That is why when pursuing an outdoor minimalism mindset with gear, packaging should not make or break your decisions.

When you are to the point of analyzing decisions to include the type of packaging, your analysis should look very similar to how you identified the product. Companies that are transparent on their sourcing for product materials often overlook the sourcing of the packaging. So as a consumer, going through the entire packaging production sourcing process might be difficult, but if possible, it should be included in your analysis. If you cannot find that information, you can always ask. After that, look at the afterlife of the packaging.

How should we define sustainable packaging? According to the Sustainable Packaging Coalition, sustainable packaging is defined as any packaging that "can be transformed into a closed loop flow of packaging materials in a system that is economically robust and provides benefit throughout its lifecycle" (Sustainable Packing Coailition, 2011). A distinction I must make within this definition is that their vision of a closed-loop system is an industrial one, meaning it fits the Outdoor Minimalist's defini-tion of a reuse system. Most industrial closed-loop systems like the Sustainable Packaging Coalition describes are largely focused on recycling and include some managed composting and waste incineration (waste to energy or energy recovery).

Common Product Packaging Environmental Impacts in Production and Afterlife

Virgin Single-Use Plastics: This is plastic, usually in the form of a wrap or a polybag of some kind that uses nonrecycled natural resources (crude oil, coal, natural gas) for produc-tion. The extraction of these natural resources involves deforestation, fracking, and oil/gas leaking. The afterlife of a single-use plastic is the landfill. If it doesn't make it there, then it will contaminate the ecosystem with microplastics as it breaks down over time.

Recycled Plastics: Unlike virgin plastic, these plastics have been recycled at least once. The recycling process still takes energy and water, but it doesn't involve the extraction of new natural resources. The afterlife of these plastics depends on what they were made into. If they are single use, they will go to the landfill or out into the environment. If they were made from a more durable or heavy-duty plastic product and into another recyclable package, then they have a chance to be used again if they are recycled.

Paper/Cardboard: The majority of paper packaging production comes from monocropping agricultural models that negatively impact soil quality and biodiversity of that specific ecosystem. Moving to pulping and paper production, chemicals like mercury, nitrates, chloroform, and benzene are used to treat wood chips but leach into the soil during processing. Air pollution from paper mills includes carbon monoxide, ammonia, and nitrogen oxide. Not all paper packaging is pure, and it can include dyes that can impact the paper's afterlife in recyclability, compostability, and even when burning. In 2014, the EPA calculated that paper products made up 26 percent (67 million tons) of the 258 tons of solid waste generated in the United States. It has also been speculated that the paper industry uses more water during production than any other form of packaging because of the extensive processing required to turn wood into paper—this includes growing, pulping, and bleaching (Haggith et al., 2018).

Hemp: can be used much like wood can but can be recycled more times than wood pulp due to durability and stiffness. Hemp is also monocropped for production but can yield more in a shorter amount of time and does not require bleaching or chemicals to complete the pulping process and overall uses less water during production. The hemp plant is useful in its entirety and has long been known for its ability to pull heavy metals from the soil, making it a great rotational crop. If no dyes are used on hemp packaging, it is easily compostable and in most cases can be recycled.

(*continued*)

Common Product Packaging Environmental Impacts in Production and Afterlife (*continued*)

Bamboo: Another common alternative to paper and plastic packaging, bamboo is a fast growing and considered a renewable resource for materials. Bamboo plants can grow in depleted soils and do not require deforestation to be farmed. Much like hemp, it does not require chemical treatments for pulping and is less often bleached. Bamboo packaging is, in some cases, compostable at an industrial level, but it can be difficult to find recycling centers that accept it.

Other Plant-Based Packaging: There are several other plant products that can be turned into packaging that are far more renewable and easier to compost. Some of them include mushroom, kenaf, coconut, bagasse, and cornstarch. Most of these can be made into a cardboard-like structure or paper to package goods. Some plant-based plastics also exist that are marketed as "bioplastics" but this is largely a marketing ploy, and they should be treated the same as standard plastic products.

SAMPLE EMAIL SCRIPTS

After surveying several outdoor companies that strive to be environmentally responsible, the consensus is that a direct message on social media or an email via the contact information on their website is the best way to communicate concerns, questions, and new ideas.

Public social media comments are a good way to raise awareness, but companies do not always read them. At least the people making decisions aren't reading all of the comment threads. Many customers have left negative feedback in social media comments that will simply be deleted or forgotten. Companies are more responsive to personal and thoughtful emails and messages. This gives them a chance to truly understand your problems, see you as a potential customer, and hear how they can be better in the future.

That isn't to say that customer reviews are not important. There is a difference between a customer review and a targeted, overly aggressive comment made on social media. Reviews are direct, whereas comments are rather passive and can be seen as unmeaningful.

When you decide to reach out to any company regarding their environmental or sustainability claims (or lack thereof), do your best to be direct and honest without shaming them. For instance, if you notice they are greenwashing something, remember that it is possible for a company to unintentionally greenwash products.

When Writing an Email to a Company

- Have a specific issue or concern. The more specific, the better. As an example, if you are concerned about the impact of the dyes they use for their tent fabric, say that specifically.

- If your concern is about a production practice or material, explain why this is an issue and provide possible solutions they can use moving forward.

- Try to do some research to find the right department or person to email these concerns to instead of jumping right to the contact box on their website. These types of concerns can get lost in all of the other emails they deal with on a daily basis, and that is not what you want.

- Represent yourself and your relationship with the company. Have you used this brand for years and are just noticing changes or discovering ways they could improve? If you are not yet a customer, also express that you would be more likely to buy from and tell your friends/family about these products if these things were more transparent or changed.

So, you bringing this information forward should be in an effort to help them see the issue and give them solutions to fix it.

Greenwashing concerns email template

My name is [your name] and I have been a longtime customer of [company name]. I've recently come to learn about the term greenwashing, and noticed that some of your company [claims, packaging, etc.] appear to be greenwashed. I was disappointed to learn this about [company name], as greenwashing is a very misleading marketing practice, whether it is intentional or unintentional.

As a leading company in the outdoor industry, my hope, as a consumer, is that all of your sustainability efforts are done in a way that are genuine and intentional which is why any form of greenwashing is deeply concerning. My intention in sending this email is to increase your awareness of the type of marketing that you participate in and reevaluate the motivation behind using misleading sustainability claims.

I will speak for all consumers and say that we expect and deserve true product transparency, especially when it comes to the sustainability of a product. I urge you to reevaluate and restructure your [claims, product packaging, etc.] to either better represent production and environmental practices or to remove the greenwashed statements completely.

Product packaging email template

My name is [your name] and I recently bought [product name]. I'm satisfied with the product and have enjoyed using it, but when I received it, I was disappointed to see that you use [single-use packaging, nonrecyclable packaging, etc.]. Have you considered using different packaging when shipping and packaging your products?

I've recently come to learn that product packaging contributes to a large percentage of our municipal waste, and I believe that we can all be a part of the solution. I'd like to recommend your product to my friends and family, but I'd also prefer to buy from a company that not only has ethical production practices but also considers the product packaging they use as well.

Material sourcing or production concern email template

My name is [your name] and I have always loved [company name] products. I've recently come to learn that you use [type of materials or production practices], and it is deeply disappointing to know that a company I've long held in high regard contributes to less than desirable sustainability practices. While I'd like to continue to support your business, I cannot ethically continue to purchase or recommend your products unless sustainability and ethical sourcing is at the forefront of your business model.

I urge you to provide genuine product transparency with all consumers moving forward so we can make informed purchasing decisions. Better yet, please reconsider your [sourcing or production] to better reflect your company sustainability messaging.

General sustainability and transparency email template

My name is [your name] and I am interested in purchasing your [product name]. During my product research and company comparisons, I noticed that you do not provide very specific information on sustainability, production practices, or sourcing of your materials. As a consumer, I will only buy from companies that make product transparency a priority. I am interested in your product as it seems to have good reviews, but I'm only willing to invest if it fits within my definition of sustainability and ethical production practices.

I urge you to provide genuine product transparency with all consumers moving forward so consumers can make informed purchasing decisions.

Don't Throw Old Gear Out

THERE'S NO DOUBT THAT OUTDOOR GEAR CAN BE EXPENSIVE, AND it doesn't last forever. Shifting out of a use-and-dispose mindset helps us to see the factors that affect durability and get creative about getting the most out of your gear. If you've always been taught that backpacks are only meant to last a year or that you need to restock every season, you might not have stopped to think about where those items come from, how long you can make them last, or where they'll end up when you toss them.

Price isn't always the biggest factor regarding how long your gear lasts. Quality, frequency and style of use, storage, and maintenance all influence equipment life span. The goal of this chapter is to give you the information you need to help keep your gear functioning longer and what to do once it is time to retire specific items.

MAKE YOUR GEAR LAST LONGER

By far, one of the most important ways to help make your gear last longer is to change your mindset when something goes wrong with your gear and how carefully you tend to that gear. It can be tempting to always be up to date on the latest equipment, but that can also subconsciously make you believe that you need to invest in brand-new gear when what you have is still wonderfully functional.

Trust me, I understand that irresistible pull to be up to date on the newest gear. I am a career outdoor and environmental writer, and I spend a fair amount of time researching gear, comparing gear, and writing about gear. All of this is interesting, and it can be amazing to see all of the new innovations and improvements, but it can also make me feel like I might *need* the newest gear because it is the *best*. Of course, I buy new gear sometimes, but I am always asking myself, "do I *need* this or do I *want* this?" The mindset of necessity shuts me down almost every time, and I revert to enjoying and preserving the gear that I currently have.

Discerning between what you actually need versus what you might want is central to any form of minimalism. Take stock of the activities you actually participate in and what you need to enjoy them safely. [Flip back to the "Get to Know Your Gear" chapter to refresh on how to identify gear you need versus gear you may want.]

When many people think of making gear last longer, they focus somewhat heavily on repairs, which we will get to later in this chapter. While in reality, the main focus should be on maintenance, intentional use, and storage. It can be very tempting, especially if you're tired from a day or week on the trail, to toss everything down and forget about it until next week, but these types of habits can wear out gear much faster.

Maintenance of your outdoor gear essentially means that you follow the manufacturer's guidelines in terms of cleaning and, for gear like knives, sharpening. Many of us rarely get around to cleaning our outdoor equipment, because it is easier to tuck things away in a closet and get to them later if we remember. The thing is, all the sweat, dirt, grime, salt, and anything else you accumulated outside can start to build up into components and fabrics causing the materials to break down, rust, and deteriorate prematurely.

While you may not think it is necessary to clean your gear after every use, it isn't a bad habit to get into, especially for gear like backpacks and boots. The environment you were in can also influence the necessity of cleaning. For instance, if you are rock climbing near the ocean, chances are, your gear has some salt on it and should be cleaned as soon as possible to prevent any damage. Your boots and other gear should also be cleaned before entering new ecosystems to prevent carrying trace elements between environments, including nonnative (and potentially invasive) plants, insects, or bacteria.

Cleaning is an important part of keeping gear in good shape, but how you dry that gear after it is cleaned matters too. For instance, certain materials should not be dried in the sun or at a very high heat because they may shrink. The same goes for when you are out on the trail. It can be tempting to dry things near the fire, but be wary about how close you get things to the fire because it can alter the gear's shape and even melt certain materials, especially plastics (including polyester).

Unless you've bought used gear, the manufacturer will provide cleaning and care instructions for you to follow (and you should follow them). If you buy used gear, use resources from that company's website. Most companies will have step-by-step care instructions or blog posts that cover proper equipment maintenance.

As a general rule, it is a good idea to wash your outdoor gear (tents, sleeping bags, outerwear, etc.) every four to five times you use that item. However, if your gear is visibly dirty or you were out in a very muddy or sandy environment, you likely need to wash that gear right away when you return. Some gear, including most synthetics, can be washed with standard eco-friendly laundry detergent. Other gear, like down or waterproof materials, often require specific cleaning solutions and may not be suitable for washing machines. Items like backpacks, with all kinds of buckles and zippers, should be washed in a bathtub.

After washing materials like Gore-Tex, rain jackets/pants, or even tents that are waterproof or water-resistant, you'll also need to reapply a waterproof coating. With or without washing, waterproof coatings wear off over time. Some gear-specific detergents will contain waterproofing and even UV protection, but if they do not, be sure that the gear you intend to waterproof is cleaned so the coating is applied effectively. Many waterproof coatings (like Nikwax or Scotchguard Water Shield) are an easy-to-apply spray and can be applied when the gear is either wet or dry: The gear simply needs to be clean first.

The same goes for applying the sealant to tent floors and seams. After you've washed a tent, always check to see if the PU coating of the floor, seams, or fly feels sticky or appears to be peeling. If you notice these things, then they should be fixed before storage or use.

Maintenance also means knowing how and when to reapply necessary coatings or applying the necessary protection. Leather boots, for example, take more frequent maintenance, but they often are a longer-lasting material if cared for properly. If you don't already know how to clean and care for leather boots, then you should learn! Proper upkeep of materials like leather ensures that they do not dry out or crack. The main considerations to make when caring for leather boots are choosing the right cleaners and conditioners for the type of leather, how to clean the boot material, how to apply the conditioner, and how to dry the boots when you're done. Since most footwear leather is either full-grain or rough-grain leather, like nubuck, read product instructions for maintenance to learn how to properly condition and clean your boots. While traditionally wax-based treatments were popular, much of the outdoor industry has switched to treating leather boots with other types of conditioners that help to restore the DWR (durable water repellent) and will not impair your ability to replace the sole of the shoe.

If you only camp during the summer and fall months, gear maintenance and cleaning may involve taking your gear out in the spring and inspecting it. Are there areas that need to have their seams sealed on your tent? Does your bivvy need a new waterproof coating? A simple inspection of your equipment before you use it and after you get back from a trip is one of the best maintenance tips when it comes to gear. Look for minor tears, gaps in seams, or places the sealant is peeling. This gives you a chance to fix any issues before you're out in the woods and before they become unmanageable.

How you are using your gear can impact longevity as well. Do you carelessly toss your pack down onto the ground when you take a break from hiking? Do you opt out of using a rope tarp when climbing at the crag? Do you just toss things into the back of the car or have no order or organization when you pack things up for storage? Being intentional with how you handle and pack your gear can impact how fast it wears down. It can also break down faster in certain areas if you always pack in the exact same way. One example of this is always putting your water bottle on one side of your pack. Now, this may seem like a small thing to consider, but that side of the pack will likely wear down faster than if you switch the location of the bottle each time you use the pack.

The same can be said for making sure that you use gear for the intended activity. This might seem like an obvious tip, because why would you do otherwise? As you get more discerning about actual gear needs and move toward minimalism, though, stretching an item's use can seem like a good idea. You may try to make one item that is meant for something else work for an activity that is far too demanding on those materials. Instead, invest in activity-specific items, especially for high-wear activities like caving, climbing, or mountaineering.

Where and how you store your gear will likely depend on space and climate. Store most outdoor gear in a dark, dry place. Moisture and sunlight can damage your gear and cause it to break down faster (not to mention the possibility of mold). Climate-controlled storage for high-value items is ideal, especially if you live somewhere humid. When possible, try to store gear in enclosed containers to prevent rodent or bug damage.

The gear itself determines how exactly to best store it. Sleeping bags are a good example—synthetic bags can sometimes stay packed without much worry, but you should always loft or hang a down sleeping bag, and I opt to loft my synthetic bag. Lofting prevents the insulation from bunching, causing an uneven fill and potential cold spots. All sleeping bags should be hung and dried for at least 24 hours after use to prevent moisture from getting stuck. When you are on a long trek, hanging your sleeping bag once you arrive at camp is a great way to keep the bag feeling fresher and staying dry.

BEGINNER'S GUIDE TO REPAIRING GEAR

You do not need to be "crafty" in order to repair your gear. It may take some of us a bit more practice and research, but with time and effort, you can easily get in-the-know about how to repair most items. A big part of gear maintenance is staying ahead on small repairs. Check your gear before and after you use it. This can help you catch small tears and rips right away. Always fix the small things before they become big things. These small things can be a seam loosening or a small tear on a mesh pocket and are usually quick and easy fixes that you can manage with a sewing kit on the trail or at home.

There may be times where a fix is too big for us to handle, or something simply malfunctions and we feel it should be replaced. Before jumping right into that mindset, do some research and always contact the company to ask about the warranty information. Many outdoor companies will offer to do repairs, some for free and some for a small fee. Other companies may also replace the item entirely, especially if what failed on the equipment was a manufacturer error. Some outdoor gear stores even have in-house repair shops. We all know you can get big-ticket items like bikes repaired, but outdoor-gear repair shops that fix items like backpacks and boots exist both online and in person. They will charge for repairs, but you can guarantee that it will be a high-quality repair and will likely be much cheaper than replacing the entire item.

If the repair needed is a bit bigger than a small tear on a pocket and you need more guidance with that piece of equipment but don't have access to a repair shop, another great resource is the manufacturer's website. Many companies, especially sustainable clothing companies, will have videos or articles detailing ways you can fix items at home.

There is no doubt that repairing your gear is often easier when you are at home, but gear can also break or rip when you are using it. If you are only on a day trip, this may not matter much, but if you are planning to be out for several days, then it is wise to get to know quick and easy fixes to get gear to at least last you until the end of your trip. Along with a first-aid kit, consider carrying a gear repair kit. Your repair kit does not need to be fancy or overly stocked, but it should include a few key items.

Not all backcountry gear fixes will be forever fixes, so that's why it can be handy if you know how to repair things like zippers or apply patches to pants when you get home. Fixing the initial issue while the gear is still in use should be a priority though, because if it is not addressed it will likely continue to worsen. Plus, you often only have one of a given item (i.e., sleeping bag) in the

Sample Gear Repair Kit

- Duct Tape (or sailing/rigging tape)
- Tenacious Tape or NOSO Patches
- Multitool
- Needle and Thread
- Super Glue
- Paracord
- Seam Sealer
- Optional Items: Extra pack buckle, tentpole splint, zip ties, glasses repair kit

GEAR REPAIR KIT

Common Gear Repairs You Can Do at Home

Tent/Bivvy Rip: Ultralight tents are especially susceptible to rips and tears, and tent floors are often the first to give out. Most small rips in a tent or bivouac sack can easily be repaired with some Tenacious Tape.

Tent Seam Leak: Patches don't work on everything, especially if it isn't a flat surface like a tent seam or the seam next to the air valve on your sleeping pad. For these fixes, using some kind of seam sealant or adhesive is necessary.

Tentpole Break: If you have a pole splint or sleeve kit, this will be the best solution when you are in the backcountry and this happens. You can also use a tent stake and some tape when in a pinch. You may also have to replace the stock cord over time.

Sleeping Pad Puncture: If you use a foam sleeping pad, no need to worry here. If you use an inflatable sleeping pad, then first, avoid putting the sleeping pad directly on the ground; use a barrier like a tarp if not in a tent. Move rocks and sticks away from the sleeping area as well. For a sleeping pad puncture, Tenacious Tape is the classic fix.

General Fabric Tear: Clothing tears are a bit trickier because they vary drastically. For some items, you may be able to fix them easily with a sewing kit and a dab of Super Glue. Other things, like a tear in the knee of your pants, may need to be patched more strategically at home. Some companies accept clothing repairs within their policies so double check that if it is a big fix. Invest in NOSO Patches for easy fabric fixes.

(*continued*)

Common Gear Repairs You Can Do at Home (*continued*)

Puffy Jacket Fabric Tear: Puffy jackets are an amazing part of any layering system in the wilderness, but they are also one of the most prone to snagging and tearing. For these small holes, use Tenacious Tape or NOSO Patches.

Backpack Straps and Buckles: Straps and rips can often be sewn back together on a backpack. Most packs will come with replacement buckles, and if they don't you can reach out to the company to get more. Try to buy from companies that have repair policies.

Shoes: The materials your shoes are made from will matter as to how you can fix them. Invest in a boot repair and cleaning kit that is specific to those materials (leather or synthetic). If the soles are separating, this is an easy fix with some shoe glue, and laces can easily be replaced. If you're unsure how to fix your shoes, look into a shoe repair shop.

backcountry, so if something breaks, you may need to know how to fix it in order for it to be usable for the remainder of your trek.

Don't forget that you don't have to repair every item yourself, and it can sometimes be better to have a gear expert do it for you. But if you can repair the item, you should.

WHAT TO DO WITH YOUR OLD GEAR

Everyone's outdoor gear gets to the point of no return where even the best repairs don't quite cut it, but that doesn't mean it should end up in the trash. This section highlights programs that recycle outdoor equipment, places to donate old gear, and other ways to ensure you have a way to safely divert gear away from the landfill.

Best to Send to the Manufacturer or Repair Shop for Repairs

Zippers: Cleaning and lubricating zippers is a great maintenance tip to prevent them from breaking, but once a zipper starts to snag or stops working, then fixing it yourself can be hard. If you need a zipper replaced, you may be able to get it fixed at a local repair store, shoe repair shop (the old-school ones do zippers), or send it to the manufacturer.

Straps/Buckles: Unless you have replacement straps and buckles, you may have to send these in to be repaired, or you can contact the company and they will send you a replacement to attach yourself.

Large Rips: Especially if you are not experienced with sewing, patching large rips in equipment or clothing is going to be difficult. Not all companies will advertise that they repair these items, so ask if they repair damaged gear and if they will replace the item or repair it for you.

Climbing Shoe Soles: While you may not be able to send the shoes directly back to the manufacturer in all cases, there are several companies that resole climbing shoes.

Bikes: There are bike shops in most major cities that have all you need to replace and fix bike equipment.

Manufacturer Failure or Malfunction: Always check the warranty and repair policy to see if the company will replace or repair items. For some companies, they will only repair items if it is a manufacturer error of some kind. In these cases, they may replace the item completely, especially if it is a recall of some kind.

If you look back to the seven Rs of outdoor minimalism, you are going to find a lot of similar themes there as you do here. When you get to a point where you feel the need to retire your outdoor gear, first, avoid putting it in the trash.

Instead, try one of these three things:

1. Reuse (or sell/donate)

2. Repurpose

3. Recycle

Ways to reuse, sell, or donate old gear

Sometimes we simply outgrow gear. That means that it is still usable and someone else may benefit from having it. Reusing outdoor gear can come from either donating or selling those items, or if you have children and one outgrows something like a pack, hold on to it until their younger sibling fits into it.

Keep in mind that if you are retiring old outdoor gear, you're likely doing so for a reason. No one wants a pack that is no longer usable. No one can use a GPS that doesn't hold a charge. Be realistic in this category and don't simply default to donating old gear to a thrift store or someone you know because you're not sure what else to do with it. Before you allow someone else to use your old gear, evaluate the reasons why you're getting rid of it in the first place. If it is because it doesn't work or function anymore, then jump to one of the next two options.

If you are upgrading outdoor gear in favor of a new product, then start looking into some local gear swaps or charities. Better yet, ask friends or family members if they'd use that gear and help them get started with an activity you love.

Most major metropolitan areas have gear swaps or used outdoor gear retailers. An amazing example of this is Ride-a-Bicycle in New York City. I have seen similar programs in other cities, like Duluth, Minnesota, where they take old bicycles, repair them, and give them to people that need them for transportation. These programs often help people of all ages get an affordable and reliable mode of transportation to get to and from work or school. Some of these programs also teach bicycle repair classes to youth and other community members. Other local used-gear shops will accept used outdoor clothing, tents, sleeping bags, etc., then repair them and resell them so they can have a new life.

One sport that is a big contributor to waste within the outdoor industry is climbing. I love climbing, and it is far from the only activity that creates waste. However, climbers go through a lot of nylon—a material that is difficult to recycle. Sports like climbing produce a lot of waste, because you really can't stretch safety equipment. At a certain point, it is no longer safe to use that gear any longer. Harnesses, ropes, slings, quickdraws, cams, etc. all have an expiration date, and that can be based on how much it is used in a season, how it is stored/cleaned, and if there were any major falls and damages. Folks who climb more than once a week might need to replace gear like ropes every single season or more to ensure safety. Other climbers that only use their ropes once or twice a year might be able to get by on a rope for 4–5 years, depending on the wear. Climbing ropes from individuals and gym facilities contribute to a fair amount of waste.

The yarn to manufacture climbing ropes is made from nylon. Part of the reason nylon is so good for climbing ropes is because it is incredibly durable with a high melting point. These factors mean it can withstand falls while you're climbing, but it makes it difficult to recycle. Nylon can be recycled, but unless the industrial manufacturer of that climbing rope is willing to take the rope back and break the nylon down, it isn't going to happen. A few rope companies (Sterling, Millet, and PMI) have rope recycling programs and may provide credit for sending in your old rope when you buy a new one.

If we can't always recycle climbing ropes though, we are left with the choice to either throw the rope away or repurpose it. If you're anything like me when it comes to old climbing ropes, you have the best intentions for repurposing it into a rug or something new. The furthest I've ever gotten with repurposing any amount of climbing rope myself is making a dog leash, but I was still left with the majority of the rope.

That's where a company like Duluth, Minnesota–based CragDog comes into play. Similar to other used-gear-collecting businesses, they will take your old climbing ropes. The difference is that they won't be reselling them for climbing use. Instead, you can send your climbing rope to them, and they'll repurpose it to become a dog toy or dog leash. Even in the roughest shape, a climbing rope (or at least most of it) can be repurposed to be strong enough to be a dog leash or a fetch toy. The mission and purpose of CragDog is to reduce the amount of waste produced by the climbing industry, especially when it comes to plastic and petroleum-based materials like ropes or harnesses.

Ways to Donate Your Outdoor Gear That Is Still Usable

- Ask friends and family if they want/need the gear you don't need anymore.
- Bring to a local thrift store, charity, or used gear shop.
- Bring outdoor clothing (especially warm weather clothing), sleeping bags, tents, etc. to shelters and charities to distribute to those in need.
- Put items up for sale online or find a "buy nothing" group online to find someone that will use and care for the items.
- Contact a local scout group to see if they have any participants that may need equipment.
- Send usable REI equipment to someone in need using their GiveBackBox program.

Right now, they work primarily with individuals, but they are also working with the midwestern climbing gym chain Vertical Endeavors to repurpose and upcycle their old ropes. They are currently expanding to repurpose old webbing harnesses to become skijoring harnesses for cross-country skiing as well. They accept old climbing ropes, harnesses, and hardware at various drop-off locations in the Midwest and by mail.

Ideas for repurposing old outdoor gear

Repurposing can also be referred to as "upcycling" and is unique to the type of gear you have. There are not a lot of ways to repurpose a GPS unless it becomes a child's toy, but for other gear including climbing equipment, packs, skis, clothes, and more, a little bit of creativity can go a long way.

Keep in mind we want to minimize the waste associated with the repurposing project. That means if you plan to turn an old climbing rope into a rug or a dog leash, consider how much new material you'll have to buy, how much of that rope you are actually going to use, and what to do with the waste. Better yet, send your rope to CragDog and let them take care of that for you.

While finding a repurposing project for gear can be a fun and exciting activity, it isn't always the best option if you end up having to toss most of the materials in the end. You can find ways to recycle the materials that you can't use in your project. In either case, consider the afterlife of those materials, because even projects with the best intentions may not always have the expected or desired outcome.

If you are going to seriously get into upcycling your outdoor gear, I recommend investing some time into learning how to sew properly. You can learn a lot of skills online these days, but nothing can really beat an in-person class or two for something like sewing. You can do most of these projects if you know how to sew by hand, but they will be much easier and faster if you have access to a sewing machine. Keep in mind that while a sewing machine is something else you'd have to buy, in the long run, it is an investment that keeps providing you with the ability to repair and repurpose clothes and gear for years to come.

One of the best ways to hone your skills is repairing gear and clothing. This gives you a chance to practice and work up to bigger projects. For instance, before you decide to repurpose your old tent, consider working on smaller projects like turning an old pair of pants into shorts or old base-layer clothing into a winter-friendly buff. Start small and do your best to find patterns to follow if you are overhauling materials completely.

Examples of Ways to Upcycle or Repurpose Outdoor Recreation Materials

Tent: Use materials to make stuff sacks, use the bottom of an old tent as a footprint for a new tent, use tentpoles when gardening for beans, if it is big enough and made from ripstop fabric you can make a hammock, or if you have kids teach them how to make a kite.

Backpacking Pack: Strip materials down and salvage what you can. One of the best things you can do is save pieces to repair your new pack when necessary, but if enough of the pack is usable, consider making yourself a daypack.

Sleeping Bag: Turn it into a quilt, repurpose it as a sleeping bag for your dog, or make it into a pillow.

Sleeping Pad: Foam sleeping pads can be used for a mat to sit on around the fire and can also be used as a makeshift outdoor dog bed. Inflatable sleeping pads are more difficult to upcycle, so you may need to get creative with them.

Bicycle Tubes: Cut them up to make rubber bands or use the materials as new handlebar tape.

A lot of upcycling comes from your own creativity and ideas that fit your lifestyle. I encourage you to think outside of the box when repurposing gear but try to have a plan in place so you are not wasting materials along the way.

How to recycle outdoor gear and equipment

Recycling is imperfect, but it is still one of the best options we currently have to divert products and materials from the landfill. In a perfect world, we would not have waste products, and recycling would be the last resort or at the very least only be for materials we can infinitely recycle, but we are not there yet and we may never get there.

Right now, most individuals, companies, communities, and municipalities see recycling as the optimal solution to solving our waste problem. In the realm of outdoor minimalism, recycling, at its best, should be seen as a Band-Aid to a much larger consumer problem (we'll learn more about recycling in the next chapter). Not to say we shouldn't recycle, but the original three Rs we grew up learning were put in a specific order for a reason. Meaning, we must first start reducing, reusing, and then if we can't do those things, we recycle.

As I step off my soapbox, if you have outdoor gear of any kind that has reached its expiration date and you have no option to rehome or repurpose this item, then please do your best to learn if and how those materials can be recycled. Even recycling, though, starts with mindful consumption and choosing gear suppliers carefully. For example, responsible companies offer take-back programs that make recycling their products easy. A few big names that run programs like this include Patagonia (Worn Wear) and The North Face (Clothes the Loop). Customers can send or drop off old clothing, and they will handle the rest. But as we have learned, a garment's life is not over as soon as it leaves your hands. Patagonia's Worn Wear program accepts 100 percent of the clothing sent back to them, but that doesn't mean that they can use all of it. They are transparent about this, and they are always finding new ways to work on creating more of a closed-loop or circular system. According to Patagonia, they recycled 6,797 pounds of materials in 2018 alone. Still, they have a stockpile of materials they can't use because they're too tattered or too smelly to be repurposed. They are hoping to find a solution for this unusable clothing to prevent it from going to the landfill or incinerator, which is how a lot of recycling technology is developed. A waste issue is identified, and when something cannot economically be recycled at the moment, it may be recyclable in the coming years as more technology and waste management systems allow.

Green Guru is an outdoor company that upcycles specific types of gear to prevent them from going to the landfill. Green Guru accepts items like old bike tubes, wetsuits, and tents to repurpose them into new outdoor gear. Some REI locations also accept old bike tubes, but you need to call ahead to ensure your local location participates in the program. Another example of this upcycling scheme is Metamorphic Gear. They accept tarps, some tent materials, and sailcloth to be upcycled into other items like bags and wallets.

Fuel canisters are a backpacking consumable we should consider recycling or refilling if possible. Surprisingly, many propane and isobutane containers marketed as single use can be refilled with the purchase of an adapter. Many consumers opt out of doing this because of laws in their country, dangers involved in refilling pressurized canisters, and the general hassle of doing it correctly and with the right blend of fuel.

The good news is that most of them are made from stainless steel, which is easy to recycle. The bad news is that most curbside recycling services don't accept stainless steel. You may need to drive to a drop-off location that accepts stainless steel, and pressurized stainless steel canisters, at that. The reason many recycling centers opt out of accepting pressurized fuel canisters like these is because of the dangers recycling and crushing pressurized fuel canisters presents to their workers. Although fuel canisters can be tricky to recycle, it is possible. In order for any recycling center to accept used fuel canisters, they need to be empty, punctured, and clearly labeled.

To do this, you need something called a CrunchIt tool (I only know of Jetboil having one of these but other brands may have similar tools) to release the fumes that remain in the can from the top nozzle. The CrunchIt tool can be used to puncture a hole into the canister, and then write "empty" with a black permanent marker on the side. Without the CrunchIt tool and the "empty" labeling, the canister will not be recycled. Recycling facilities need these clear markers that the canister is safe to recycle, and they will not have their employees investigate unmarked canisters for safety reasons. Instead, unmarked canisters will be thrown away.

Putting the refilling or recycling of these canisters on the consumer is potentially dangerous and often leads to a collection of nearly empty canisters in your garage or more likely, all of them being sent to the landfill. It would be nice to start to see fuel companies offer an exchange program, empty canister recycling drop-off locations, or refillable options. These are not the only type of fuel available, but they continue to be commonly used. Lower-waste options, like liquid fuel stoves, are refillable.

Other stainless steel camping equipment like cooking pots and water bottles can also likely be recycled, but you will need to contact your local recycling center to see if they accept those materials and if you can put them in the curbside pickup.

A popular company known as Terracycle has become known for their ability to recycle things we used to never imagine we could recycle, and they may have come to mind as you were reading this section. However, they do not accept outdoor gear for their recycling services. They do accept some food wrappers, such as energy bar wrappers, which we will discuss in the next chapter.

The issue with recycling, in general, is that there is not necessarily a universal system of any kind. When it comes to outdoor gear recycling, you kind of have to use your ability to problem solve, research, and ask questions. Although I only mentioned a few companies in the recycling section here, there are several other companies that make tents, sleeping bags, and other products that may accept old gear and participate in either a repair or recycling program of their own. If you're unsure about what to do with your old gear and repurposing or repairing it isn't an option for you, contact the manufacturer directly and see if they accept the materials back.

Bonus Tip: Cloth made from 100 percent cotton, hemp, or merino wool can be composted, but only if it is not mixed with any synthetic materials. Contact your local composting facility about their capabilities or process and compost the materials at home.

USED GEAR: TRASH OR TREASURE?

One of the most significant barriers to outdoor recreation is the price of gear. To both combat a sense of elitism and the environmental impact of always buying new gear, buying used outdoor gear and equipment has gained popularity. Across the United States, more and more gear consignment stores are popping up, and large outdoor stores like REI also run Good & Used online retail sales.

Stores like the Great Lakes Gear Exchange in Duluth, Minnesota, the Durango Outdoor Exchange in Durango, Colorado, Outdoor Gear Exchange in Burlington, Vermont, Wonderland in Seattle, Washington, and the Boise Gear Collective in Boise, Idaho, have begun to set a new standard in a few major outdoor hubs when it comes to gear. After talking to one of the Great

Lakes Gear Exchange owners, it is clear that in many outdoor communities, a barrier to entry remains, and gear consignment challenges the idea that you need the newest, latest, and most expensive gear to thrive outdoors. Instead, gear consignment gives beginners and experts alike a way to play safely outdoors at an affordable price.

Anyone toying with the idea of opening a used gear store should consider that community support can make or break your business model. Running a consignment store, especially for outdoor gear, will be an individualistic experience and mainly based on the clientele of that area of the country. It is hard to know everything about every piece of gear, and it is essential to be humble, ready to learn. A great way to build community and a brand before you decide to open is to start small with event pop-ups and online shops. That way, you get a feel for the community's interest and build a brand your community is excited to support. After all, as told by the Great Lakes Gear Exchange team, selling used gear can't happen if you don't have a community ready to sell their old gear to you.

Not every community is the same, and not all outdoor sports are popular in all places. So, owning and operating a used gear store is variable according to your location and the time of year. Depending on how the store is operated, they may not have an extensive inventory, and instead, might only invest time into selling high-quality, lightly used gear from reputable brands. As a consumer, when you are buying used gear, it can still be tempting to buy based on price, but the brand, materials, and warranty should also be a consideration. Even if you buy used gear, certain brands will have a lifetime warranty for a particular product, meaning that they'll still honor the warranty even when it switches owners. Other brands always honor repair policies on their equipment as well, so company research is just as important when buying used gear as when buying new if you want something that will last.

Since most of these community-owned and -operated used gear stores operate with consignment store business models, they do not accept gear that is too torn or ripped. That makes it difficult for some people to donate damaged gear, but it still opens up the door to those who are simply upgrading their gear or getting rid of something they no longer use. When visiting Duluth during the summer of 2021, I decided to take a look at the Great Lakes Gear Exchange. The gently used, reasonably priced gear they had in stock and the store organization made it feel like a traditional outdoor retail store. I ended up buying some bike panniers I'd been shopping for online, saving me some money and the transit of shipping that item to me (win-win).

Used gear isn't always a black-and-white shopping experience for consumers. It can take longer to find the items you are look-ing for, and you may not find what you want at all. Although you can still buy plenty of used gear online, the benefit of a local gear exchange is that you still have outdoor enthusiasts there to help guide you through the process of buying gear. Much like going into a traditional outdoor retail store, the staff is on hand to help you find things and answer questions.

Used gear isn't a cure-all for our addiction to new gear in the outdoor industry, but it is a great place to start. Used gear can help level the playing field, empowering more people to pursue outdoor sports, and divert more materials from landfills. I've been to a number of outdoor-focused cities, but very few seem to have a used gear store of any kind. And when I attended university in Duluth, it always surprised me that there were not more options for buying outdoor gear in town. The Great Lakes Gear Exchange has only been open for a couple of years now, but the community support has been astounding, which further points to the fact these types of gear exchanges are needed in active outdoor communities.

One unfortunate reality of the outdoor industry is that some of your outdoor gear is going to end up in the landfill and that's all there is to it. You can do your best to lengthen the life span of your gear, but unless it can be recycled over and over again, the eventual afterlife is trash. This specific outcome is the primary reason why mindfully lessening consumption is at the forefront of outdoor minimalism.

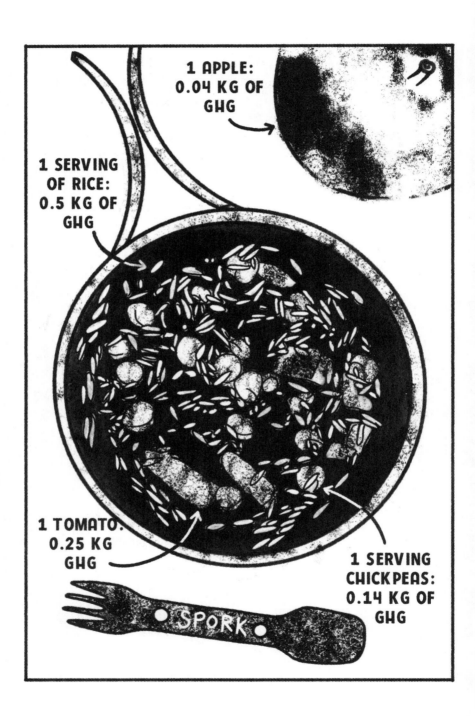

Rethink Trail Food

FOOD IS CENTRAL TO THE PLANNING OF ANY TYPE OF OUTDOOR expedition. After all, your food is your fuel on the trail. It should be nutritious, easy to prepare, and ideally, environmentally friendly. For many, choosing what you eat based on the environmental impact, especially for something like backpacking, may seem like an unnecessarily narrow focus. Like with our daily lives, when we only take the face value of what we are eating based on convenience, we are missing a big piece of the puzzle regarding where our food comes from and the impact it has on the planet (and our bodies).

Once you start looking into where your food comes from, you will quickly learn that the environmental and social impact of food production is not equal. Accessibility to information regarding nutrition and impacts of our food system has increased, but even the most accurate information can become clouded with opinion and persuasion as the driving focus. I'm not here to tell you what to eat, but I am here to invite you to think critically about your trail food as a part of our global ecosystem and arm you to make informed decisions about your environmentally conscious diet.

When you are choosing sustainable trail food, the main aspects you should be considering include:

1. Origins of the food

2. Impact of that type of food

3. Packaging production and afterlife

ORIGINS OF FOOD

First, let's consider how the food is processed and, more specifically, where that food is grown. Knowing where your food comes from adds an element of connection and appreciation. Some readers may immediately gravitate toward images of a personal garden or even picking berries on a local trail when they are in season. Summertime is often a time of abundance when it comes to our food. There is a special satisfaction and appreciation that comes from picking perfectly sun-ripe tomatoes, foraging greens, and cutting up crisp cucumbers fresh from the market to make a summer salad. That close connection to our food is rare, though.

Unfortunately, not every meal can be garden-fresh, especially when it needs to be portable and nonperishable for the trail. Long-distance food travel is essentially the norm within our current model of food production, especially for packaged and processed items. Food miles are a complex measure that helps us to quantify the environmental impact of how far food travels from producer to consumer—accounting for each ingredient and mode of transportation. Air transportation is often far more energy-intensive than other methods of transportation (Pirog and Benjamin, 2005).

It is extremely difficult to determine the average number of miles food travels because of how many factors are involved. Still, Iowa State University's Leopold Center for Sustainable Agriculture and the ATTRA Sustainable Agriculture Program conducted studies about the environmental impact of the food distribution system and the average food miles traveled. Although the Leopold Center for Sustainable Agriculture has been a leading researcher for food miles, the most prolific study they conducted was in 1998, making it hard to know how accurate those numbers are today. Regardless, the study is often cited and referenced when calculating food miles and is used as a model for calculating food miles. That's why there's a chance you've read in some major news outlets (e.g., the *New York Times*) that, on average, food in the United States travels around 1,500 miles. This isn't necessarily an inaccurate number, and it is close to one of the calculations the Leopold Center for Sustainable Agriculture found in their study. Unfortunately, choosing just one number to represent food miles is an oversimplification of the food distribution system.

Expecting a consumer then to identify food miles along with sourcing and nutrition is a big ask and nearly impossible unless it is clearly labeled and identifiable. So, if food miles aren't simply listed along with nutritional information, how are you supposed to determine the impact of a food item? Eating and sourcing food locally is often hailed as the best option for consumers when trying to lower their greenhouse gas emissions. But why is eating and sourcing food close to where you live so important?

According to the 2008 Farm Act, local food is defined as food that is sourced within a 400-mile radius of you. However, many people only consider food within 100 miles as locally sourced. Whatever your radius, local food means that the food is being transported a shorter distance and you are able to potentially have a better understanding of the production process of that food. Most of the time, when referencing eating locally, people are talking about fruits and vegetables. Some of these are great trail foods, apples or oranges for example, but you likely aren't going to be packing freshly picked tomatoes or salad greens.

You can choose to shop locally for produce and dehydrate or preserve the foods to make backpacking meals yourself (jump to the end of this chapter for directions). Where you live and the climate you live in will drastically impact your access to local foods. Finding local food isn't always as easy as going to the grocery store, and farmers' markets do not run year-round in all parts of the country. Not all grocery stores effectively stock local foods, so for many consumers, the inconvenience of finding local food often outweighs their attempt to minimize greenhouse gas emissions of food miles.

Find Where to Buy Local Food Where You Live

- Look at produce stickers and product packages to see if a place of origin is listed.
- Ask grocery stores where they source certain products from and if any of it comes from within a 400-mile radius.
- Contact or visit the local farmers' market.
- Research if there are any CSA (community supported agriculture) programs near you or if there are any food co-ops you can join.
- Contact local gardeners, especially ones that write newspaper columns. They often know where to get local food or where to take classes on gardening.
- Post an ISO (in search of) post on your social media, in area groups, or even on craigslist and look into food waste reduction smartphone apps like OLIO.
- Look into online food directories like Local Harvest, Eat Well Guide, or the USDA Agriculture Marketing Service.

Other Ways to Reduce Your Food Miles

- Eat less processed foods and foods with less packaging. Sticking to whole foods reduces the amount of processing and ingredients, which reduces collective food miles.
- When eating meat, stick to locally/organically raised or local/legal hunting.
- Buy extra of your favorite fruits and vegetables when they are in season and get into preserving (dehydrating, freezing, canning).
- Invest time in gardening. If you don't have room for a garden, look into a community garden plot.
- Talk to local politicians about a local food policy council if it doesn't already exist.

(Hill, 2008)

Preparing everything you eat on the trail isn't always a feasible option, so you may plan to buy premade meals or prepackaged backpacking meals. If that is the case, then similarly with gear, look into company practices and where that food originates. Looking at an entire meal, such as those made by Mountain House, for example, it becomes increasingly difficult to pinpoint where each and every ingredient originates. Yes, you may be able to find a local company or at least a company within the same country as you that makes backpacking meals, but where are they sourcing those ingredients?

Unless you are growing, collecting, and processing all of your backpacking food yourself, then you are going to need to do a little digging into where the companies you are buying from are sourcing their ingredients. Much like with gear companies, if you are looking for sustainability information of any kind, the first place to look is on the company website. If you are struggling to find anything about food sourcing, send them an email to ask. If they don't reply to that email, move on to the next option. The easiest way for any company to get away with unethical or less environmentally friendly practices is to keep their consumers in the dark. So, if you are asking questions and are not receiving a reply, they likely don't want you to know.

There are some smaller companies popping up here and there that focus specifically on producing backcountry meals using sustainable packaging and local foods. For example, if you live in the Pacific Northwest, the Fernweh Food Company produces dehydrated plant-based meals sold in low-impact packaging and using only seasonal local ingredients. This is just one example, so if you are struggling to find local foods or local premade back-packing meals, other outdoor enthusiasts in your area are a great resource. Get to know the community, ask questions, and you may be surprised what you can find.

IMPACT OF TYPE OF FOOD

The food we eat both on and off the trail has an environmental impact. Although eating local food may be ideal, it isn't always going to be an option. So, whether you are buying prepackaged meals or buying ingredients from the store to make your own meals, get to know the impact of the food itself.

Food miles alone do not account for the entire life cycle of that product. The environmental impacts of food cannot solely be based on distance traveled, but should also include what happens throughout the entire production, transportation, and distribution process. A study from 2008 concluded that food miles and transportation only accounted for 11 percent of our food's greenhouse gas emissions (Weber and Matthews, 2008). Another study from 2011 found that an even smaller percentage (6 percent) of our food's global greenhouse gas emissions came from transportation (Gustavsson et al., 2011).

Climate solutions often hyperfocus on clean energy, but the more digging you do, you'll learn that over a quarter of global greenhouse gas emissions come from food production. When talking about food production, we can break it down into a few categories to help identify major players and percentage impacts of each category (Poore and Nemecek, 2018):

- Livestock and Fisheries = 31 percent
- Crop Production = 27 percent
- Land Use = 24 percent
- Supply Chain = 18 percent

Each of these categories is broken down into smaller sections; for instance, the crop production can be separated between crops grown for livestock consumption and crops grown for human consumption.

Eating locally is wonderful, but it can only do so much. Consumers may in fact have more of an impact if they focus specifically on *what* they are eating versus *where* it is coming from. No doubt, transportation contributes to greenhouse gas emissions, but that is only one piece of the puzzle. As consumers, we can attempt to shift our mindset to see the bigger picture of where emissions are coming from within the supply chain. We must account for the land-use change, the farming of those animals or plants, animal feed (if livestock), processing or slaughter, transportation, retail, and packaging.

That's a lot of information to process when you're trying to buy some oats and powdered milk for an upcoming expedition, but trust me, it gets easier with time. One big part of integrating a minimalist mindset into your life is not feeling obligated to change all of your habits at one time. An all-or-nothing attitude can work for some people, but for others, that is an unsustainable mindset that can easily become overwhelming. Strive for progress, not perfection, use what you have, and consider changing one thing at a time.

When looking at the impact of industrially produced products, across the board, animal-based products have higher greenhouse gas emissions. It's not just CO_2, either—agriculture also contributes large amounts of methane and nitrous oxide to the atmosphere (Ritchie and Roser, 2020).

Cured beef is common, nonperishable, protein-rich, portable trail food, and beef alone has the largest impact of animal agricultural production. So, let's consider beef a little more closely. One of the most startling comparisons of the impact of animal protein and plant protein is between that of beef and peas. Just 1 kilogram of beef raised in industrial conditions like a Concentrated Animal Feeding Operation (CAFO) produces 60 kilograms of greenhouse gas, while 1 kilogram of peas only emits 1 kilogram of greenhouse gas (Poore and Nemecek).

Yes, this is just one example, but overall, the study concluded that animal products most often emit more greenhouse gases than plant products. The data they collected was taken from more than 38,000 commercial farms in 119 different countries. For most of the products that they looked at, the largest impact of measured greenhouse gas emissions was a result of land-use change and farm processes such as fertilizer application, manure management, and enteric fermentation (methane production in cattle stomachs). Nearly 80 percent of the emissions came from those two stages, while the remaining emissions came from processing, transportation, retail, and packaging.

Well, you might ask, what about sustainably raised cattle that are slaughtered and processed locally? Surely that still counts for something since they aren't being raised in a CAFO environment? After all, most studies like the one mentioned above are looking at global impacts of protein-rich foods, not necessarily small, family-owned or sustainable farming models. These are great questions in terms of the environmental impact of your food, but the answer may not be what you're looking for. Since the farming process is responsible for 80 percent of emissions, buying from a local beef farmer doesn't do as much in terms of minimizing your carbon footprint as avoiding beef altogether. Sustainable cattle farming is potentially a better option in terms of animal welfare and regenerative practices than intensive, factory farms, but in almost all circumstances, *eating less meat* is going to produce fewer emissions than simply eating *sustainably raised* meat.

It is true that most data collected on this topic can feel skewed because it focuses on industrial, large-scale farming. Other factors like intensity of animal population, geography, opportunities, environmental laws, pasture quality, and general land management all play a role (Gerber et al., 2013). Animals sourced from smaller farms will, in general, have a slightly lower greenhouse gas impact than industrial farms, but they will still have a higher amount of land usage, water usage, eutrophication (extra nutrient pollution of ecosystems from farms), and greenhouse gas emissions than even the most resource-intensive plant products (German, Thompson, and Benton, 2017).

It is up to producers to employ responsible environmental practices. All consumers can do is do their best when it comes to their individual decisions and their situation. With all this information and more studies being released regularly, I personally adopted a plant-based diet for the sake of the environment. Concern for the animals themselves has made being vegan an easy commitment for me to keep and uphold as a lifestyle. I'd love to see a world where animal farming is abandoned altogether, but that is not a realistic expectation, and that mindset can often hold back progress by driving a wedge between movements with similar environmental goals. You don't have to go vegan or be fully plant-based, but you do need to learn how to make informed decisions about where your meat is coming from and/or seriously consider reducing your consumption. Try alternate sources of protein like nuts and legumes. Experiment with one meatless meal a day or a meatless day a week. Look into local farmers that are trying to raise animals more sustainably, visit their farms, and get to know their animals. Replace beef with chicken or fish. Raise animals of your own if you can. Find a mentor to teach you how to hunt and process the meat yourself. The bottom line is to get to know your food, where it comes from, and who it is coming from, in order to begin to remove the cognitive dissonance and expectations of immediate gratification of our current consumer culture.

Okay, so how does all of that apply to trail food? Essentially it applies in the same way it applies to your daily diet. Focus on where your food comes from and the impact of that particular product, and begin to replace some animal proteins with plant proteins. It is going to be very difficult to nail down and identify where each and every ingredient came from when you are buying a premade backpacking meal unless the company is putting in a direct effort to inform the consumer of their sustainability practices. So, sometimes hard decisions must be made and habits must be changed. Processing your own food and preparing your own trail meals is one of the most effective ways to have a closer relationship with your trail food and to ensure that you are aware of the impact and origin of that food. However, that is only realistic for certain types of expeditions and won't always be an option for thru-hikers and bikepackers who are getting food on the go. In these situations, there needs to be a broader look at the impact of food beyond locality and packaging. Sometimes it won't be an option to avoid waste, so we must then start to look at where we are able to minimize our impact in the moment.

Like any other product, food can easily be greenwashed and often is by using labels and unregulated terms that appear to be environmentally friendly. For example, why did I just contradict everything we discussed about food origins by telling you to avoid "locally grown" labels? The thing is, locally grown is an unregulated certification and can be applied to almost anything. There are not specific enough parameters for this certification, just like

What to Look For When Buying Food at the Grocery Store That You Intend to Dehydrate or Preserve for Backpacking Meals

Look for certifications like USDA Organic, Rainforest Alliance, Marine Stewardship Council, Non-GMO Project Verified, and Fair Trade Certified.

Avoid certifications or phrases on labels like free-range, pasture-raised (unless paired with Animal Welfare Approved), 100 percent natural, and locally grown.

there are no rules regarding the use of the word *natural* on food labels. If you are trying to buy local food, look to see if the farm and location is disclosed versus solely trusting the certification.

Also keep in mind that animal products can also be organic, hormone-free, and antibiotic-free. These are reliable certifications, but just because you are buying beef with those three certifications does not eliminate the environmental footprint it has. Certifications can help you start to narrow down which foods to choose from, but they need to be considered along with the bigger picture of the entire food production process.

Food Packaging Production and Afterlife

The third consideration when it comes to choosing a low-waste food product is likely the one that you've thought about the most: the packaging. The reason packaging is often the first thing we look at when moving into a low-waste lifestyle is because it is tangible to us. We see it when we buy the food items, and we have to do something with it when we are done. The other two aspects of origin and general impact of the food are more ambiguous and feel further removed. Most readers probably do not live near a factory farm or in a rural farming community, and they have never seen the direct impact of industrial farming. But we have all seen foil wrappers littering the trail and neighborhood parks. Much like when considering the product packaging of your gear, the food packaging may not always be avoidable and should not be the only determining factor in your decision.

Regardless, packaging is a piece of low-waste living that should be a consideration, and it is hard to get around when you are looking for nonperishable and packaged goods to take into the backcountry. Most backpacking meals come in single-use disposable bags, and other foods we love on the trail like energy bars or trail mix come prepackaged as well. There are many times when avoiding all food packaging while backpacking is impossible. In those situations, it is often more effective to choose a plant-based option rather than no packaging because of the entire life cycle and impact of that product throughout production.

According to the Environmental Protection Agency (EPA), packaging and containers make up the majority of all municipal solid waste in the United States. Statistics from 2018 showed that around 82.2 million tons or 28.1 percent of total waste generation in the United States came from food packaging and containers. When gathering this information, they categorized packaging and containers as the materials used to package or protect goods for sale. This included food, beverages, cosmetic products, medications, etc. They also included the materials used in the shipping and storage of goods. The rate of recycled packaging has increased dramatically since the 1960s, but so has the amount of packaging materials produced and used. The report states that only about half of all of the packaging material waste produced in 2018 was recycled. The rest was combusted or sent to the landfill.

Yes, this calculation does not strictly include food waste packaging, but a large percentage of all packaging and containers sent to the landfill does come from food packaging. Think about how much food you buy in 1 week versus the number of other products you buy, then consider the packaging associated with both. On average, food packaging is likely taking up more room in your trash bin than other types of packaging. In an ideal world, we would not be worrying about what to do with food packaging waste because it would either not exist or fit into a circular system. Unfortunately, we live in a very imperfect world filled with single-use packaging that can feel near impossible to escape. So, what are we to do?

Most of the packaging waste within the food industry is happening before a product ever reaches us. After all, we don't have much of a choice when it comes to the packaging the food we want to buy comes in unless the company is considering consumer and environmental demands. When we are working on eliminating food packaging waste at either a consumer or

Steps to Eliminating Food Packaging

1: Track and Assess

2: Implement Waste Reduction/Prevention

3: Evaluate Disposal Strategy

production level, the steps to take are relatively similar, but they are applied at a different scale.

These three steps can be applied within any area of your life, but I find them most helpful in the realm of food and packaging waste. Like any other aspect of an outdoor minimalist lifestyle, don't feel obligated to change everything overnight. Avoid an all-or-nothing attitude and implement small changes until they become healthy habits. Then, you can move to the next step.

The type of adventure you embark on will also influence this process. For instance, a cross-country bike tour or thru-hike will produce far more trash simply because it is harder to pre-make and prep all of the food you will need for the trip. That's why changing what you can when you can is the best way to implement lasting changes and create more mindful consumption. As you are planning for the next outdoor expedition, actively think about how you can plan your trail food around these three steps in an effort to reduce your food packaging waste.

Step 1: Track and Assess

Before we can make a change in our food waste or food packaging waste, we need to know what areas need changing. Tracking and assessing essentially means the first few times around, you go about your business as usual when it comes to trail food. Buy what you usually buy and eat what you like when you are on the trail. During that process, take notes and track all of it.

For example, if you are going on a weekend backpacking trip, make a meal plan (jump to page 102 to see how). Then, when you go grocery shopping, save your receipt so you have a record of what you purchased. This next step may seem strange, but save *all* of the food packaging. You may put some of your trail food in different resealable containers before your trip, so find a box or bag to save those packages. While you are hiking, you are likely already carrying your trash and not leaving it on the trail.

When you get home from your trip, get a towel, lay it on the floor, and put all of the food packaging (including plastic bags you used to separate food items) you used for that trip out onto the towel. While this step may *feel* unnecessary and looking at trash is a bit awkward, I find it to be a powerful exercise. It gives you a visual representation of the waste produced during just one of your trips. It is tangible and prevents the instant "out of sight, out of mind" experience we often have with disposable food packaging.

Next, while you have the packaging out on the towel, get ready to take some notes with your phone or a notepad. Look at the individual packaging and take note of what it is made out of and if it is compostable, recyclable, or must go to the landfill. When doing this exercise you can also evaluate if you had any food waste from your trip. Knowing how much food you actually need for an outdoor trip can help save you some pack weight and avoid food waste on future adventures.

Companies can use a similar approach, but it will be on a much larger scale. They won't be laying their packaging waste out on the ground, but they can gather general information regarding operation processes, collect data for all waste produced through production, and then analyze areas for improvement.

Step 2: Implement Waste Reduction/Prevention
Once you have collected a baseline of data for the amount of food packaging waste produced during a trip, start looking at areas

SUBSTITUTE WITH TRASH LESS SNACKS LIKE GRANOLA OR DRIED FRUITS!

GATORADE POWDERS CAN BE BOUGHT IN BULK!

CONSIDER BUYING NUTS + SNACKS IN BULK

OATS CAN BE BOUGHT IN BULK AND PRE-SPICED TO YOUR TASTE.

THINK ABOUT MAKING YOUR OWN TRAILMIX

THERE ARE MANY HOMEMADE DINNER RECIPES THAT CREATE LESS TRASH

TRY BRANCHING OUT AND INCORPERATING DIFFERENT PLANT BASED OPTIONS.

THINK ABOUT A DEHYDRATED OPTION (LESS WEIGHT + TRASH)

for improvement and changing purchasing and trail food habits. Remember, everything you consume, whether it is food or packaging or product-related, comes from somewhere. By reducing the amount of food packaging you use, you are reducing greenhouse gases and energy used to make that packaging and transport those materials. On top of that, if you are reducing or refusing product packaging, even just sometimes, that is one less food wrapper that is intended for the landfill or that is littered on a trail.

Unless you are growing, processing, and packaging all of your trail food yourself, then you are going to have some food product packaging. You can minimize the amount of packaging by buying food products in bulk or from bulk bins and using your own containers, but this is not an option for everyone. If it is available, buying from bulk bins to make common trail snacks like trail mix, energy bars, and even your own backpacking meals is the best low-waste option.

If that is not a possibility, and you are buying prepackaged backpacking food, you will have to deal with the waste that comes with that. For most outdoor enthusiasts, this is going to come in the form of energy bar wrappers, backpacking meal pouches, and other packaged snacks. Most of this packaging is made of plastic of some kind and may have an aluminum lining. The combination of these materials makes the packaging difficult to reuse or recycle for anything, and most of the time, the intention is for it to be put in the trash. In these scenarios, the company is valuing convenience over sustainability.

If you completed the first step in tracking and assessing your food packaging waste, then you can look back at your notes and start to replace high-waste packaging with lower-waste options. To do this, look at the packaging materials. Is it made of plastic? Is that packaging recyclable in the area you live? Ask targeted and realistic questions to help you identify the pieces of packaging that you feel have the biggest impact and rank them.

Then, make another list to identify the foods that are easiest to replace with lower-waste options. For instance, can you get oats in a bulk bin? Can you make your own granola bars? This is going to look different for everyone, because we all have different lives with varying incomes, time constraints, and accessibility to food items. We may not all have time to devote to making all of our own trail food, and that's okay. That's why I recommend making two lists: ranking packaging based on impact and ranking packaging based on ease of replacement. Compare these two lists to each other and make a final decision as to which packaging to change first. There will be some overlap between your lists, but if you are just starting to reduce waste in your life, make the easiest and most accessible changes first. Small successes lead to powerful results in mindset and will empower you to make larger, more impactful changes in your future.

An example of implementing a change like this is instant oatmeal. Oats for breakfast is a classic outdoor meal, and many of us are likely familiar with the single-serve pouches of instant oatmeal. Let's be honest, these are uber convenient and filled with the carbs and sugars we want and need during outdoor expeditions. They require minimal work to pack and all you need is some boiling water to make breakfast. They are packaged in some kind of paper with a wax lining. Seems harmless, right? Sure, compared to the plastic energy bar wrapper, but it might be the most realistic replacement for you to start off with when planning your next trip. Buy oats in bulk if you can, pre-mix any toppings you'd miss from the instant stuff, and pack a reusable heat-safe dish. No bulk access? Compare the waste of one canister of quick oats or even a package of muesli with the number of individual wrappers wasted with instant oatmeal packets, and you'll see a clear winner. Any waste reduction is good waste reduction, whether it is paper, plastic, or anything else.

Ways to Implement Waste Reduction Strategies

- Identify food items that can be purchased in bulk.
- Package your own food in reusable containers or wraps instead of plastic or single-use bags.
- Find similar food items that come in home-compostable or recyclable packaging.

Step 3: Evaluate Disposal Strategy

When buying prepackaged food items for an outdoor expedition is unavoidable, take time to look at the packaging and if that packaging is recyclable or at-home compostable. As you may know, items that can be recycled have a triangle shape made of arrows with a number to represent it is recyclable. Unfortunately, most consumers ignore the number and assume the recycling symbol means it can go into the recycling. Those numbers actually matter.

A friend of mine used the term "wishcycling" recently, and I believe this perfectly describes the primary mentality many of us have surrounding recycling. We often wishfully put materials into our curbside recycling bins and hope they end up properly recycled. Some of the time we aren't even sure if the item is recyclable, but we put it in the recycling anyway. We adopt an "out of sight, out of mind" mentality and assume that the recycling system in our area has the environment's best interest in mind. Unfortunately, most municipal recycling services look at budgets before they consider the long-term impact of our failing recycling system. Theoretically, municipalities sort and sell recycled materials for at least enough money to cover the cost of recycling operations. When supply and demand get out of whack, though, recycling doesn't make economic sense and often becomes cost-prohibitive.

In so many ways, recycling is a complex issue that has become increasingly difficult for consumers to follow because there is no streamlined process. Not only that, but at the end of 2017, China stopped accepting recyclable materials from countries like the United States (Tita, 2018). China used to import and process around two-thirds of the world's recyclable materials. Before the ban, many countries including the United States, Japan, Germany, and the United Kingdom, shipped around 8.8 million tons of plastic annually to China for recycling (Brooks, Wang, and Jambeck, 2018). With China's decision, the United States had to essentially restructure their entire recycling program overnight, and much of that burden fell onto local governments. Since local municipalities are often in charge of recycling, there are noticeable differences in the focus and effectiveness of recycling programs across the country. In fact, there are some areas that omit recycling altogether simply because the cost is far too high to maintain in comparison to sending all material waste to the landfill.

The unfortunate truth behind recycling is that it is not going to save the planet, and as a 2020 Greenpeace Report on plastic recyclability states, "most types of plastic packaging are economically impossible to recycle now and will remain so for the foreseeable future." We are falling short on recycling and reuse claims during every step of the production, distribution, and waste management process. As a consumer, this can be an overwhelming thought, because although something may be labeled as recyclable, a recyclable label may be a false promise sold from companies to consumers. By putting the brunt of our waste onto recycling, we are giving ourselves a false sense of accomplishment in our move toward environmental repair. In my eyes, using recycling as a fallback simply helps us justify our consumer-based actions as opposed to changing them. We are putting too much faith in a system that can no longer ethically support the current model of recycling and consumerism.

How these concepts can be integrated into your life will look different for everyone, but be realistic about the long-term impact of the packaging once it gets picked up off your curb. To do this, you need to know and understand what the recycling numbers mean and which numbers are recycled in your area.

In general terms, most local municipalities will accept numbers 1, 2, 4, and 5. It is much rarer to find a recycling center that accepts 3, 6, and 7. Most food packaging made from aluminum, glass, and paper—if they are a stand-alone material and not mixed—will be accepted, but these may not have numbers. These regulations and the numbers accepted vary from location to location, so you are going to have to do some research into what numbers are accepted in your area. If you are purchasing packaged food for a trip, try to look for packaging that is actually recyclable where you live or are traveling.

Since many trail food packages do not fall within those categories, the next best option is to look into Terracycle programs or similar local systems. Terracycle is a program that works with companies to recycle hard-to-recycle materials (e.g., food packaging). For instance, Mountain House meals, Clif products, and GoGo SqueeZ packages have recycling programs through Terracycle. Like all recycling systems, Terracycle isn't perfect, but they are doing amazing things and working hard to close a gap in the current recycling model we use. For most of the items they recycle, they have consumers clean packaging, let it dry, and mail it to the closest Terracycle location. Cleaning product packaging for recycling should be a habit all consumers get used to no matter what type of recycling program they use.

As a consumer that is looking for "green" ways to reduce their impact, you may also be looking to see if the packaging you're buying is made from recycled materials. Buying products made from recycled materials is a great habit to get into, especially if you can find 100 percent recycled packaging. Read the entire statement regarding the packaging product material though. When

Recycling Numbers and What They Mean

#1 PETE or Polyethylene Terephthalate	Plastic beverage bottles and select food packaging
#2 HDPE or High-Density Polyethylene	Opaque plastic bottles or jugs like detergent bottles, milk jugs, cleaning product bottles, or cosmetic bottles
#3 PVC or Polyvinyl Chloride	Commonly used material for PVC pipes, but also used to make shampoo bottles and wire jacketing
#4 LDPE or Low-Density Polyethylene	Plastic films like shrink-wrap or plastic bags but can be used for squeezable plastic bottles
#5 PP or Polypropylene	Container for hot liquids due to the high melting point, and used for medicine bottles, plastic syrup bottles, bottle caps, and straws
#6 PS or Polystyrene	One of the most versatile plastics and is used to make things like packing peanuts, take-out containers, CD cases, egg cartons, and plastic cutlery
#7	The grouping of the rest of the materials that did not fit into the other six categories. Most local municipalities do not accept recycling number seven because it is filled with so many miscellaneous items and materials.
#20-22 PAP or Paper and Paper/cardboard	Used for general product packaging as a sleeve or a box
#40 Steel	Can be used to make food cans
#41 ALU or Aluminum	Used for some food cans, drink cans, and aluminum foil
#70 GL or Clear Glass	Used for some drink containers, but generally used for food jars

Pre-Consumer Recycled content: packaging made from materials collected as manufacturer waste and never made it to the consumer. These materials may be collected from scraps, rejects, or trimmings of products made or any leftover materials that end up on the factory floor.

Postconsumer Recycled content: packaging made from recycled materials that a consumer disposed of in a recycling process of some kind. These materials often include items like food cans, drink bottles/cans, paper products, and other easily recyclable packaging materials.

products are labeled as "up to 50% recyclable materials" it could be anywhere from 0 to 50 percent of that packaging was actually made from recycled materials. Another phrase that is often used to define recycled packaging materials is either pre- or postconsumer recycled materials.

Both pre- and postconsumer recycled packaging is better than buying packaging made from virgin materials. Both can be labeled next to the recycling symbol with the letters PC, PCR, PCW, PCF, Pre-C, Post-C, or the phrase "recycled content." They may also simply state next to the recycling symbol "made from [pre or post] consumer recycled [materials or content]." To trust these statements, it should also state that it is third-party certified to ensure it uses those types of materials for packaging.

Composting is another way to reduce packaging waste. If you live in an area that has an industrial composting facility, this process is going to be much easier. There are several food packages that can be composted in industrial facilities but cannot be composted in at-home garden compost. This is why looking at the packages closely for certifications is an extremely important step in understanding how to dispose of waste most effectively. There is an at-home composting certification, but if a package simply states that it is compostable with no other context, it is safe to assume that it must be composted in an industrial facility.

Some Common Terms Used on Packaging to Represent "Compostability" or "Biodegradability"

Bioplastics: Similar material to plastic, but made from a biomass of some kind like corn, potato starch, or soy proteins. Not all bioplastics are biodegradable, but in comparison to standard plastics that are fossil-fuel-based, they are carbon neutral if they break down.

Biodegradable: Some materials that are labeled as biodegradable, are biodegradable (e.g., paper). However, you will also see biodegradable plastics as packaging. Biodegradable plastics can break down, but only by living organisms (bacteria) in the correct environment. Biodegradability standards for plastics within this category require that the materials end up as carbon dioxide, methane, and water. These biodegradability standards only work if those materials are sent to an industrial facility that can create the proper environment for the material to fully break down. In the wrong environment (landfill, litter, etc.), "biodegradable" plastic materials simply become microplastics.

Compostable: Similarly to biodegradable packaging labels, many materials labeled as "compostable" can only be processed in industrial facilities. The intent behind composting is to have the material break back down into humus (the organic components of soil) and return to the earth. A package labeled as "compostable plastic" must be directed to the proper industrial composting facility, as it will not break down without proper conditions, just like biodegradable packaging.

At-Home Compostable: A newer certification rising into the packaging scene is at-home compostable. This is by far the most trustworthy certification to look for because it means what it says: You can compost the materials in your garden compost with minimal issues. For most of these materials, you will need to cut them up or shred them to help them break down effectively. Keep in mind that at-home compostable packaging should be composted when possible—it won't break down very well or as effectively when sent to the landfill.

We must understand that as consumers we are not fully aware of all label requirements or certification qualifications. That's why when we are assessing the waste we produce from food packaging, we also need to evaluate the capabilities of the waste management system where we live. Certain packages labeled as "compostable" may seem good in theory, but unless you have access to an industrial composting facility, your efforts will be in vain. Research the best alternatives to those items and start by mitigating what it is you are consuming versus trying to manage disposal as an afterthought.

At this point, you may be wondering what materials you *should* be looking for in food packaging. Should you try to get a material that is recyclable or compostable? How do you know what the options truly are and their impact?

The answers aren't always simple, but those are the types of questions we need to be asking. It means that we are thinking critically about our choices and are starting to see that everything we do as humans has an impact on the world around us. The primary issue with food packaging is that most of it is designed to be single-use, and as we have learned, recycling and composting claims are not always to be trusted. Similar to the resources and materials used to make outdoor gear, every piece of packaging uses energy, water, and chemicals to be produced, and is rarely entirely reusable or truly recyclable.

With all of that background information regarding the packaging your trail food comes to you in, go back to the two lists you made earlier to start applying this knowledge. For instance, perhaps you can buy more items in aluminum cans or only purchase packaged foods from companies that participate in a Terracycle program. There is a catch to all of this though, and that is not putting the packaging over the impact of the food itself. That may mean that you are going to end up cutting or replacing several of your trail staples during this process. In finding alternatives to my old staple trail foods, I've often found options I enjoy far more

Materials Widely Used
for Food Packaging

(*Note:* Not all of these will be brought along backpacking but you may buy bulk containers made of these materials)

Aluminum: Aluminum is made by mining bauxite and smelting it into alumina. To complete this process, an extensive amount of energy and water is used and along with the aluminum material, greenhouse gases, polycyclic aromatic hydrocarbons, wastewater, and sulfur dioxide are also produced. The positive of aluminum (and steel) is that it is infinitely recyclable, and around 75 percent of all aluminum ever produced is still used (EPA, 2007).

Glass: To make glass packaging, burning fossil fuels are necessary to melt feedstock materials. During this process, the feedstock (the raw material used in a processing plant) is vaporized and recrystallized creating fine particulates containing heavy metals. Other pollutants from the combustion of fossil fuels create greenhouse gases, nitrogen oxides, and sulfur oxides. Food and beverage glass can be recycled over and over again, and making new glass containers from recycled glass is often cheaper than producing new glass from raw materials (EPA, 2021).

Plastics: Much of the plastic produced in the United States comes from feedstocks made from natural gas processing or crude oil refining, meaning that all seven types of plastic polymers used for food packaging are derived from fossil fuels. Plastic manufacturing is responsible for around 1 percent of greenhouse gas emissions in the United States, along with other toxic emissions like sulfur hexafluoride, nitrogen oxides, hydrofluorocarbons, and perfluorocarbons (Posen et al., 2017). The EPA estimated that in 2018, around 14.5 million tons of plastic containers and packaging materials were generated in the United States. Within that amount of packaging produced, the American Chemistry Council calculated that 13.6 percent (two million tons) of plastic containers and packaging were

(continued)

Materials Widely Used
for Food Packaging (*continued*)

properly recycled, 16.9 percent were incinerated, and the rest (over 69 percent) was sent to the landfill (EPA, 2018).

Paper: While paper and other biomass materials are often hailed as environmental saviors of the packaging industry, we must remember that while they are often a better alternative to plastic, they still have an impact on the environment. To make paper and paperboard, wood must be billed into pulp either mechanically or chemically. Other plant fibers can also be used (hemp, straw, etc.) with a similar process. Paper mills use an extensive amount of water and energy during processing and production. In the United States, paper mills no longer emit toxic wastewater, but there are still air emissions such as sulfur dioxide, nitrogen oxides, carbon monoxide, and volatile organic compounds. Paper packaging makes up a large portion (23 percent) of trash generated annually in the United States, and in 2018, around 68 percent of paper was recycled to make new paper products, making finding products made from recycled paper easier ("Industrial Environmental Performance Metrics, Challenges and Opportunities," 1999).

What About Reusables?

If you look back to the "Get to Know Your Gear" chapter, you will recall the comparison between Stasher bags and Khala & CO. These types of reusables have essentially become the face of the zero-waste movement as their mission is to eliminate single-use packaging waste. Reusables are effective, but only if we use them enough times to counter the resources used and pollution caused during their production. The overall environmental impact of a single-use wrapper might actually be lower than a reusable one if you only use that reusable a handful of times. That said, if you use the reusables, whether it be a food wrapper or a water bottle, on a regular basis, you may have a positive impact.

while being more eco-friendly during the entire life cycle. New food options add more variety to our lives outdoors, and it can feel good to make conscious choices as we build new habits.

BACKCOUNTRY MEAL PLANNING

Whether or not you are attempting to implement low-waste approaches to your backcountry food, I highly recommend always having a meal plan. I must admit that I have been there, scrambling to go on a last-minute trip, running out the door, stopping by the closest grocery store (or gas station in desperate and fast-paced times), and making do with what I had. There were times when I packed way too much food and other times I wished I had more.

If you've never done this, good for you. I don't recommend it. My number one recommendation to anyone planning a backpacking trip is to make a meal plan. Break down any dietary needs, pick out meals and snacks, and then decide how to approach the ingredients for each meal. This process does not have to be complicated. Being ready and organized with all the food you actually need will also make the trip much more enjoyable.

If you're not sure how to start making a meal plan for your trip, check out the sample below. You can easily write this out on a piece of paper or, if you are planning a trip with someone who doesn't live with you, make a shared Google document or iPhone note and edit together.

The food listed in the following sample meal plan would be meals and snacks I'd consider for one of my backpacking trips. I do not mind eating the same meals or snacks for most of the trip. More variety tends to require more planning and likely more packages, unless you can find most of your supplies in bulk bins. It may seem tedious, but it does help to plan out everything you're going to eat during your trip. The sample on the next page is for a weekend backpacking trip of 2 nights and 3 days. You can easily add or take days away and add or remove sections.

Sample Meal Plan Template

Meal	Day 1	Day 2	Day 3
Breakfast	Muesli: buy from bulk bins or a large package	Muesli	Muesli
Lunch	Bean Burrito: buy dehydrated refried beans from bulk bins + pack of small tortillas*	Bean Burrito	Bean Burrito
Snacks	Trail Mix Granola Bars Apple Dried Dates Peanut Butter	Trail Mix Granola Bars Dried Dates Banana Chips Peanut Butter	Trail Mix Granola Bars Dried Dates Banana Chips Peanut Butter
Dinner	Chili Mac: elbow mac noodles, vegan cheese powder/sauce, dehydrated chili mix	Couscous and Curry: Moroccan couscous and dehydrated curry mix (includes chickpeas and vegetables)	Quinoa, Lentil, and Kale Stew: dehydrated cooked quinoa, dehydrated cooked lentils, coconut milk powder, kale powder, dehydrated onion, spices (curry powder, veg bouillon, salt)

*Some local Mexican restaurants that make tortillas in house will allow you to order bulk tortillas and pick up using your own containers.

Once you have the meals, snacks, drinks, and other food items planned out on your trip, break them all down into individual ingredients. For example, if you are going to have a burrito bowl one night, you might need rice, beans, dehydrated onions/peppers, dehydrated vegetables, and spices. Then, decide if you are planning to buy all of these items individually and combine them to make meals or if you are going to use premade backpacking meals. Unless you are buying items from a bulk bin or have prepared dehydrated foods on your own, a premade meal can be more time effective but isn't always the most environmentally friendly option due to the type of packaging and the food sourcing.

Prepping your own trail meals not only gives you control of the flavors and perhaps more variety of meals, but it also gives you control over the impact that food is having if you have done your research and have awareness of food origin, impact, and packaging afterlife.

PREPARING TRAIL FOOD

Preparation and planning is everything. An unfortunate truth about a lot of low-waste lifestyle changes is that they can take longer and can be less convenient. However, the reward is great, and as you find systems and routines that work for you, it becomes second nature. I've found that as you integrate more and more minimalist lifestyle changes, everything means more to you, and time spent preparing for a long-awaited backpacking trip becomes a part of your trip as you build excitement for the adventure ahead.

While you are considering the environmental implications of food, you are likely also thinking about the price. If you have a tight budget, the good news is that buying in bulk and investing time into dehydrating your own food is going to be far more cost-effective than premade dehydrated or freeze-dried meals. The same can be said for making your own energy bars and trail mix.

The fastest and easiest way to integrate low-waste trail food is to work with the bulk food you have available to you. Take note

Pros and Cons of Prepackaged Backpacking Meals vs. Making Dehydrated Meals

Prepackaged meals

- **Pros:** less planning, quick cooking times, convenient
- **Cons:** more expensive, difficult to recycle packaging, not easily personalized, not always the best tasting, more preservatives

Homemade meals

- **Pros:** easy to personalize, you decide flavor complexity, you portion for your needs, can buy foods in bulk, generally cheaper
- **Cons:** you provide the packaging, takes more planning and prep before trip, can take longer to cook

of the bulk foods at neighborhood grocery stores and then make your meal plan around those options. You can also choose to do a combination of bulk foods and dehydrating some food items. Even the most minimal bulk food areas in grocery stores include awesome trail snacks like nuts and dried fruit.

Another option if you backpack often and don't have much access to a bulk food section that provides dehydrated foods is to order bulk freeze-dried or dehydrated foods online. Some major big box stores may have canisters of freeze-dried food or meals as well. Buying the individual ingredients in large portions and then combining them to your liking with spices is another alternative to buying a premade backpacking meal.

If you are going to dehydrate trail food, invest in a dehydrator. In the spirit of mindful consumption, I am not recommending that everyone goes out and gets a dehydrator right away. Before you make this purchase, decide how much you are realistically going to use it and if it is worth the investment. If you only plan to use it once or twice a year, it doesn't seem like a necessary purchase. However, if you plan to use it for outdoor trips and as a way to eliminate food waste in other areas of your life, it can be a worthwhile investment. There is a wide range of food dehydrators to choose from starting at around $30 and going up from there. Much like with your outdoor gear, don't forget that you can find items like this secondhand. I have a food dehydrator that my brother found at a rummage sale for $10, and it works amazingly well.

That's not the only option either; that's just the standard electric dehydrating method. Some foods can be dehydrated in a conventional oven, or you can also use a solar oven to dehydrate foods. Air dehydration is also an option, but is primarily used for herbs and teas.

How to Dehydrate Food for Backpacking

Luckily for the foodies out there, most food can be dehydrated. You will not be missing out on much when adding this skill to building your trail menu. The only things you cannot safely dehydrate are dairy products and high-fat foods (e.g., avocados, some meats, eggs). As a good rule of thumb, it seems best to avoid dehydrating most animal products, but some lean animal protein is okay. Most fruits can be dehydrated quite easily after cutting them up, but vegetables and meats should be cooked before dehydrating.

When preparing the food to dehydrate, cutting it evenly is important to ensure that your timing is right and the food is properly dehydrated. When dehydrating fruits and vegetables, a thickness of ¼ to ½ inch is ideal. You don't have to peel everything you dehydrate, but sometimes peeling something like apples does impact the overall texture, and depending on what you are using them for (snacking vs. in oats) you may want a different texture.

If you plan on dehydrating foods regularly and want to extend their shelf life, then you should consider adding preservatives to them. Yes, not ideal, but it does help them last longer (minimizing potential waste) and can improve flavor. I really only recommend doing this if you dehydrate foods in bulk when they are in season and plan to keep them around for months at a time. If you are dehydrating foods specifically for a trip, this generally isn't a necessary step. Preservatives to look into include ascorbic acid, citric acid, fruit juices, and sodium bisulfite.

Although it is common to dehydrate herbs and you can also dehydrate nuts/seeds, for the purposes of this book I am only going to cover how to dehydrate fruits, vegetables, meats/fish, and legumes/grains. As a disclaimer, I have never actually dehydrated meat or fish because of my dietary choices, so that information was collected from another source.

Dehydrating fruits

When choosing fruits to dehydrate, try to pick out ones that are ripe. If they are overripe or bruised though, they may turn black while drying. So, cut off any bruising if you notice a lot of it. Ripe fruit tends to have a higher sugar content, which means sweeter snacks and better flavor. If you are not peeling the fruit, make sure to wash it thoroughly before cutting and coring the fruit. Then, do your best to slice evenly. You can use a food processor or a similar kitchen appliance to make cutting evenly easier.

Once you have everything prepped, lay the pieces out on the dehydrator. Be sure no pieces are overlapping or they will not dehydrate completely. Most fruits dry anywhere from 135 to 145 degrees Fahrenheit (57 to 63 degrees Celsius), but look up temperatures for the specific fruit you are drying. If you are drying multiple types of fruit, try to pick ones that fall within the same temperature and time range so you can optimize your time and electricity use.

Drying times for fruits will range from 6 to 36 hours depending on the type of fruit. Some fruits will need to be checked periodically (every 2–3 hours) to rotate trays. In general, when drying apples, bananas, and peaches the range will be shorter and anywhere from 6 to 16 hours, whereas other fruits like grapes and pears can take up to 36 hours to dry. Be sure that once you have started drying fruit, you do not add anything new until the batch you have started has finished. This goes for all food you dehydrate, because if you add something new, the old batch may absorb moisture and take longer to finish.

Dehydrating vegetables

A positive of drying vegetables over fruits is that they do not take quite as long, but they do tend to spoil at a faster rate. When prepping vegetables to dehydrate, do your best to remove bruises, bad spots, and any rough bits of stem. Like with fruit, cut them into similar sizes and of the same thickness. Most vegetables should also be blanched before drying. To cut vegetables more easily use a food processor as you did with fruit. You can also use a spiralizer for some vegetables.

Most vegetables can be dried at a temperature of 125 degrees Fahrenheit (52 degrees Celsius), except tomatoes and onions, which should be dried at 145 degrees Fahrenheit (63 degrees Celsius). The drying time will often depend on the size of the pieces you cut, but in general, you can expect vegetables to take anywhere from 4 to 10 hours to dehydrate. Unlike with fruits, you may not want to mix and match vegetables as you dry them, especially if they have a strong aroma or flavor because as they dry, that flavor can influence the flavor of less aromatic vegetables. Things like onions, hot peppers, and brussels sprouts are a few examples of vegetables to dry independently.

Dehydrating meats and fish

As mentioned, you cannot safely dry dairy products or overly fatty foods. That means that you should only be looking to dehydrate lean cuts of meat or low-fat types of fish. You should not dehydrate high-fat foods because the fat causes the food to go rancid and spoils quickly. From what I've gathered, you also should almost always avoid dehydrating pork products because of this, but some people have had luck with sliced or cured ham products.

Much like fruits and vegetables, try to cut meat and fish into evenly sized pieces so they dehydrate at the same speed. All meat and fish should be cooked before dehydrating. Do not dehydrate raw meat products. Do your best to remove as much fat as possible if there are fatty portions of the meat. Once spread out on the trays, meat and fish will be dried at 145 degrees Fahrenheit (63 degrees Celsius) and will take around 6–12 hours to fully dehydrate.

Dehydrating grains, pasta, and legumes

You can also dehydrate grains, pasta, and legumes to help speed up the cooking process when you are in the backcountry. This is not a necessary step to take when preparing food for backcountry cooking, but if you want everything within your meals to cook at the same rate, it is advised. When you are dehydrating a grain or pasta of any kind, cook as you normally would and then dehydrate it.

- **Rice/Quinoa:** Dehydrate at 125 degrees Fahrenheit (52 degrees Celsius) for 5 hours. For your reference, about 2 cups of cooked rice/quinoa equals out to around 1 cup of dehydrated rice/quinoa. You may need to break them up because they clump as they dry so check periodically.

- **Pasta:** Try to only cook pasta to al dente if you are planning to dehydrate it to get a better cooking experience in the backcountry. Once cooked, drain liquid and spread onto dehydrating trays. Do your best to spread the noodles evenly and with minimal overlap, but this may only work for short/shaped noodles. For spaghetti or long noodles, twist them into multiple nests and place them onto the tray. Pasta should only take 2–4 hours to dehydrate at 135 degrees Fahrenheit (57 degrees Celsius).

- **Beans/Legumes:** The process of how you dehydrate beans is going to depend on whether you start with dried beans or canned beans. Follow the process for soaking and cooking if you use dried beans (pressure cooking recommended). If using lentils, simply cook them accordingly. Once the beans are cooked or if they come in a can, drain them and rinse. Spread them evenly on the dehydrator trays and dry them for 6–8 hours at 125 degrees Fahrenheit (52 degrees Celsius).

Now, if all of that seems like way too much work or you just don't have time to portion out all of the ingredients separately, don't fret. You can also dehydrate entire meals in a batch. To do this, all you have to do is cook the intended meal for your trip and

More Tips for Dehydrating Entire Meals

- Avoid fatty foods, so cook without butter, oil, and dairy if you plan to dehydrate. If there is meat or fish, they should be lean cuts, and avoid pork.

- Make sure all vegetables and meats are cut or shredded into small pieces of roughly the same size.

- Spread food out evenly onto the trays and declump as they cook (most relevant for grains).

- Dehydrate at 130 degrees Fahrenheit (54 degrees Celsius) for 2–8 hours depending on the ingredients. Check periodically.

- Allow food to cool completely before packaging and dividing into single servings.

- Label and date each bag with a description of the meal contents.

- Store in a cool, dry place, and then take it out when you are ready to leave on your trip. If you are doing this with leftovers, and want to save them for future trips far into the future, store meals in the freezer.

then put it into the dehydrator. This makes it easy to portion and season just the way you like it.

Do your best to use reusable containers to transport backpacking meals into the backcountry to cut down on packaging. The container you choose will be different for everyone and should fit their preferences. Single-use plastic bags are easy, light, and can be used more than once; however, they often can only be used at most five times in the backcountry until they are compromised. Invest in a reusable food wrapping or package of some kind if you plan to go on this type of backpacking trip frequently. Remember, reusables are only really effective if we are using them with a high frequency.

FOOD WASTE IN THE BACKCOUNTRY

Whether it is a day hike or a weeklong excursion in the backcountry, there are going to be some things you don't eat. Some major food waste items on the trail include peels from fruits and vegetables or shells from our favorite trail snacks like pistachios. My guess is that readers are going to be polarized on this issue of what to do with this type of food waste. Some of you are going to say, "toss it into the woods! It's biodegradable or an animal can enjoy the rest of that apple core."

The first group *isn't* wrong. After all, in the proper conditions and environments, your apple cores and banana peels will break down over time. But just because something is biodegradable doesn't make it okay for us to toss it into the woods and let nature do its thing. Think of your food waste as "organic litter." Although we may only think of inorganic materials as litter, like energy bar wrappers or toilet paper, we need to extend that thought to food waste (including chewing gum).

For the purposes of living a low-impact and outdoor minimalist life, litter can be defined as "waste that is discarded incorrectly or in the incorrect location." Within this definition then, organic waste is, in fact, organic litter when we toss it into the woods. I don't want to beat you down into thinking that because you've tossed an apple core or two into the woods, you are a litterer and that you need to step into the middle of the shame circle, but I do want to encourage you to reconsider your thought process to prevent you from doing it again. For most of this information, awareness is key as we move toward prevention.

Organic litter and food waste are natural and can decompose, but those that are familiar with composting know that in order for organic materials to break down fully, they need the correct environment and balance between carbon and nitrogen. Certain environments can create this, and that is what we see happening naturally on the forest floor with organic matter becoming humus over time. If you live in a humid climate, organic litter does have a better chance of decomposing, but it is going to happen far slower than you imagine. In more temperate climates or desert biomes, these organic materials take even longer to decompose because of the lack of moisture.

According to the Deschutes Land Trust, here are the average decomposition rates of frequently tossed organic litter:

- **Banana Peels:** up to 2 years
- **Orange Peels:** 6+ months
- **Apple Cores:** about 2 months
- **Pistachio Shells:** 3 years or more

Remember, these decomposition rates are highly dependent on the environment where these organic materials are littered. The primary factors that impact the decomposition of organic litter include exposure to sunlight, amount of rainfall or moisture, temperature, and elevation.

If it isn't going to decompose very fast, an animal will likely come along and eat it, so it's okay, right? Wrong. Have you ever heard the phrase, "a fed bear is a dead bear"? Well, this applies to other animals as well. If you have been to some of the most popularly visited viewpoints in National Parks like the Grand Canyon or Zion, then you'll know that feeding animals or leaving organic waste for animals to eat is an issue. I've had ground squirrels and chipmunks come right up to me expecting me to feed them in those parks. While this is cute and I love animals, it should not be happening. Wild animals should not be fed, and this behavior is unnatural and dangerous. You may know that your dog can get sick from eating certain foods like chocolate. The same applies to other animals. I don't know what wild animals should and should not eat, and therefore, I should not be providing them with foods that could make them sick or dependent on humans passing through the area. For some animals, eating foods they're not used to digesting can cause issues that can lead to premature death due to an inability to process salts, or starvation during winter months when fewer humans are tossing food out for them to eat.

Another issue with any type of litter, including organic litter, is that it invites more litter. When you are hiking along and you see orange peels left off to the side of the trail, especially if you're a novice hiker, this suggests that it is okay to do that too, leading to more and more litter in that area. What should you do with your organic waste then? Treat it as you treat other types of trash: If you pack it in, pack it out. Carry an extra bag with you and put those peels and shells into the bag to be disposed of when you are done with your time on the trail. (This is a great repurpose if your Stasher bag has a hole and you can't use it for food anymore.) When carrying food or waste in areas where bears live, you should use a bear canister or bear bag. Some campsites may provide bear boxes. Follow best practices for the area, and never feed or approach wildlife.

If you are backpacking, you can also consider burning some of the food waste if you have a fire (e.g., leftover oats) or digging a cathole to bury food waste as you would bury human waste. However, I do not encourage the cathole method although it is commonly used as a form of garden composting. The reason I don't necessarily recommend it to all people is that you have to do it right for it to work. For all waste, a cathole needs to be at least 6–8 inches deep and 4–6 inches in diameter. For those reading this that have dug a proper cathole, you know this takes some effort (especially with rocks and roots and clay in an area), and it isn't realistic to do that for a single banana peel on a day hike.

WHAT ABOUT WATER?

Another large part of your planning for any outdoor adventure is hydration. For day trips, it is more than likely that you will start off by carrying all the water that you need. For longer expeditions and multiday backpacking trips, finding water sources along the way becomes necessary. Filtering or treating water from natural sources is required to avoid illness—for yourself and even for your pets.

I never recommend carrying multiple single-use water bottles. Pack in reusable water bottles that you've filled and refill them as you go. Some thru-hikers swear by the use of Smartwater bottles, and these are quite light and durable. This isn't necessarily a bad choice, especially if you plan to use the same bottle for the duration of your multiple-month hike. Still, there are other longer-lasting options that serve the exact same purpose, are more durable, and are a similar weight.

Since water is such an essential part of staying safe in the wilderness, having quality equipment and water treatment should be a top priority. There are a wide variety of water treatment options available, and they all have their pros and cons.

Boiling is the lowest-waste option, but it's an easy one to mess up if not timed correctly, and it requires either fire or the use of your stove. I think of boiling water as an emergency water treatment option or one used only at camp. The other methods of water treatment are far more convenient for treating water throughout the day, not just when you've stopped for the night.

Water filters are hit or miss. There are so many on the market, and quality is vital. Not only should they be durable and easy to

Boiling Water

- **Pros:** Reliable, requires minimal extra gear
- **Cons:** Requires stove or fire, time-consuming, does not remove sediment

Water Filter

- **Pros:** Removes sediment effectively, generally long-lasting
- **Cons:** Adds some pack weight, not all filters get rid of viruses, susceptible to freezing, more components

Chemical Treatment

- **Pros:** Easy to use, very effective, minimal pack weight
- **Cons:** Longer wait time for treatment, can have an unpleasant flavor, does not remove sediment

UV Treatment

- **Pros:** Removes viruses as well as bacteria and protozoa, easy to use
- **Cons:** Electronic and not usually very durable for extended backcountry use, does not remove sediment, does not work if the battery dies

use, but they should also remove viruses, bacteria, and protozoa. When shopping for water filters, always check to see what exactly they filter out—many do not remove viruses from the water. Water filters tend to take up the most room in your pack and have the most working parts of any of the other water treatment systems. This gives you more gear to carry, take care of, and keep clean. The good news is that there are several water filters designed for outdoor use that with the right maintenance and, if you don't lose them, will last you for years.

One of the easiest ways to narrow down your options from the get-go is to look at the ease of use. Look for systems that use a minimalist design and just make sense. Water treatment isn't something you want to easily mess up or have the gear fail when you're in the backcountry, so also consider durability. The durability of the water filtration system you choose will often come down to the materials used. The cost of quality gear can be shockingly high, which can make outdoor sports feel slightly elitist at times, but water treatment is one area where you do not want to skimp.

One example of a high-quality, fairly priced, and eco-conscious company that sells water filter systems is CNOC Outdoors. They have a wide variety of gear, but let's focus primarily here on hydration. CNOC Outdoors is an extremely transparent brand—a key prerequisite to trust that reveals both positives and negatives. Much like we should not hyperfocus on food packaging, it is important to make well-rounded decisions regarding which companies we support and the equipment we invest in for outdoor use. CNOC Outdoors produces easy to use, functional, lightweight, durable, and repairable products. Their water bladders are designed to allow for use with several water filters beyond the ones they sell. This concept alone is very telling, because they understand that the consumer should not have to get rid of a water filter that is entirely functional to have a useful water container and filtering system.

Something unique about the CNOC Outdoors water containers and filtering system is that it does not have any unnecessary components. They've capitalized on the simplicity of design, making easy-to-use products using fewer materials. The two downsides consumers may see to their water hydration bladders specifically are (1) they're made from thermoplastic polyurethane and (2) they manufacture some products in Portland, Oregon, and others in China. These two things alone may be a complete turnoff for some shoppers, but remember that brand sustainability is not about perfection; it is about intention. This brand is imperfect, but they do offer product quality, transparency, repair policies, and B-Corp certification. The materials may not be the *most* eco-friendly, and it sucks they don't manufacture fully in the United States. But before jumping to conclusions, we have to ask ourselves why they are choosing to do those things. Some companies, especially smaller companies, do not have a choice. Larger manufacturers and other more localized supply companies won't work with a company unless they have a big enough demand or a deep enough pocket. So, in some cases, that company has no choice but to pick and choose where and when they can truly implement the most sustainable options available to them.

I spoke with representatives of CNOC Outdoors who shed some light on how they view and implement sustainable practices as a company. They view sustainability as an ongoing process, not an end state. They frame their products through a lens of sustainability by asking themselves if there is a more sustainable option. For example, they mentioned that they'd recently replaced plastic shipping envelopes with product packaging that is fully recyclable. Although they're happy with this change, they continue to look at other, better options like postconsumer materials or reusable packaging to try to avoid single-use materials and minimize their footprint. This same mindset informs their products as well. The materials used to make their hydration products are robust plastic designed to last far longer than any other hydration option on the market today. Their materials for their trekking poles are manufactured locally within the Pacific Northwest, but their hydration products are sourced overseas. To combat an afterlife in the landfill, they refurbish their water containers when possible and work with a local recycling center to recycle those that cannot be refurbished. As a rule of thumb, outdoor equipment companies should always monitor their carbon footprint and have a life cycle assessment. Life cycle assessments help companies track and adjust products and processes to reduce their environmental impact for the entire life of the product.

CNOC Outdoors is just one of many water filter system companies. I chose this example because their product is unique in its versatility and their company's values exemplify the idea of outdoor minimalism. It is true that they are not perfect, but it is impossible for a company of any kind making consumer goods to have no impact. They can simply look critically at each step of their supply chain and process to create and improve upon sustainability goals.

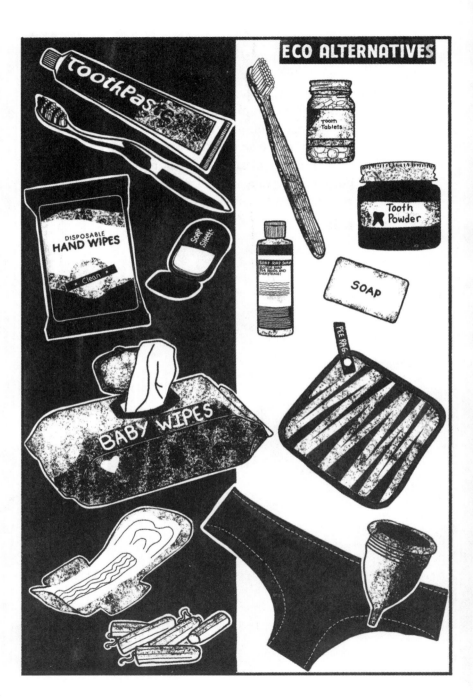

Nearly Zero-Waste Toiletries

MUCH LIKE TRAIL FOOD, TOILETRIES ON THE TRAIL ARE PRIMAR-
ily packaged consumables. First, you need to know the necessary
toiletries to bring into the backcountry, and then you can move
out from there. As with gear of any kind, identifying your needs
will be the foundation of your choices.

In this chapter, I will not only cover what should be included
in a low-waste backcountry toiletry kit, but I will also detail
ingredients to look for or avoid in products we use outdoors.
Once you're in the backcountry, you'll also need to know what to
do with these products and how to dispose of them in a way that
lessens your overall impact on that particular ecosystem. I will also
discuss emergency and first-aid kit items in this chapter.

Note: As with all other products that you buy, it will be helpful
to refer back to the "Get to Know Your Gear" chapter of this book
to review entire life cycle processes and ways to identify greenwashing while shopping.

WHAT SHOULD YOU PACK?
Backpackers tend to either bring more than they need into the
backcountry or don't bring enough. Striking a balance between
packing too much or not enough is all about identifying your
needs, and it applies to every aspect of your packing list. As with
any relationship in your life, if you don't know your needs, things
will fall apart eventually.

How exactly do you identify your toiletry needs for camping or backpacking? Much like we did when assessing and tracking your trail food, start with your preexisting habits. You need awareness of your current practices before you can begin to change and adapt to new ones. That advice only works if you have experience in the backcountry.

Where do you start if you've never created a toiletry packing list for camping before? Take heart, because it's actually easier to create environmentally friendly habits from the start than change old habits. Be realistic and mindful of your comfort zone, but also realize that you do not need all of the same creature comforts you use at home when you're in the wilderness. Things like makeup, deodorant, mouthwash, or even a hairbrush are not necessary in my experience.

Defining our hygiene and toiletry needs in the backcountry will be a relatively personal journey. For instance, in my day-to-day life, even when I'm not in the backcountry, I don't wear deodorant, so it is easy for me not to bring deodorant when I go backpacking. Not all of these habits will work or be comfortable for all readers, and that's okay. But to start identifying necessary items to pack, be aware that an unwillingness to try new things or change old habits will hurt your movement toward a low-waste lifestyle.

Identifying what you need to pack for toiletries then comes down to determining what at an individual level is required to make you feel safe and secure as you're camping, but also recognizing that your level of comfort will be different. Other aspects will play into this, like doing a thru-hike versus a weekend car camping trip. The intensity and type of trip impact how much you can pack.

Steps to Identify What Is Necessary to Include in a Backcountry Toiletry Kit

- Assess and track what you use for hygiene regularly. If you already have a toiletry kit for backpacking, assess and track waste within that kit.
- Make a list to identify and rank your perceived necessity of items. Do this before evaluating based on waste or product impact.
- Make a list to identify and rank waste created by each item on your list.
- Compare your lists to one another and see where they overlap. Are there items that can be eliminated based on waste created and your perceived value?
- Begin to narrow down your list as much as you feel comfortable, and for items you can't eliminate, make a note to look for replacements.
- Reference the Outdoor Minimalist Nearly Zero-Waste Toiletry Packing List to see what I view as necessary items when backpacking. Use this list as a reference point only or baseline, and don't be afraid to adapt it to your personal preferences and needs.

Outdoor Minimalist Nearly Zero-Waste Toiletry Packing List

When you're deciding what you *need* to pack within your toiletries, refer to the list below and modify it accordingly.

☐ Toothbrush and toothpaste
☐ Hand sanitizer and soap
☐ Trowel or wag bag
☐ Toilet paper + bag to pack it out
☐ Lip balm
☐ Sunscreen
☐ Bug repellent
☐ If needed: prescription medications
☐ Assigned female at birth: pee rag and menstrual items
☐ Optional: hand/dish towel

Notice how few items are on my list. That's because, especially when backpacking, you should only be bringing what you need and what you can carry. When car camping or in an RV, your toiletry list may be more extensive.

FINDING LOW-WASTE PRODUCTS THAT FIT YOUR NEEDS

Once you've made a personalized list for the type of trip you are taking, then you can start looking for low-waste replacements for the traditional items you may have been using. When it comes to consumables like toiletries, I suggest that you look at the ingredients first, because you'll be leaving their runoff—from washing dishes, washing your hands, and spitting out toothpaste—in the wilderness, directly impacting the environment. Not only do you want to avoid unnecessary chemicals for your health, but you need to ensure the ingredients of the products you're using are eco-friendly and biodegradable.

Not all soap is biodegradable. Some easy to find biodegradable soap options include:

- Dr. Bronner's Castile Soap
- Campsuds
- Sea to Summit Wilderness Wash
- Coleman Camp Soap

Identifying eco-safe ingredients

To preface the importance of using biodegradable soaps in the wilderness, it must be said that any use of soap, bio or not, will have an impact. If you want to truly minimize your impact on the environments you are backpacking through or camping in, omit the use of soap. In the interest of reality and hygiene, biodegradable soaps are a great alternative. Still, it must be acknowledged that soap and human interaction of any kind with a landscape has an impact. Our goal is to minimize our impact not only when using the products but along the entire production process.

Biodegradable soap is not the only concern within our backcountry toiletry kit, though. Other products like our toothpaste, sunscreen, and bug spray can contain harmful ingredients. Ingredients like preservatives or chemicals can inhibit the growth of certain microorganisms and are toxic as they accumulate in our bodies as well as in natural ecosystems.

As a general rule, go with the ingredients you recognize and can identify. Now, this isn't always the case because not everyone will know what something like bentonite clay or diatomaceous earth is, but with some research, you'll learn they are natural ingredients, which is one of the requirements when looking for biodegradable ingredients in soaps, toothpaste, sunscreens, and bug repellents. You will notice that many of the unnatural and toxic ingredients are likely things you can't pronounce unless you are a scientist or have a similar background. That's a telltale sign that those ingredients should be avoided not only for the health of the environment you use them in but also for your health.

Although the soap you may be using is biodegradable, what this means is that it has the ability to decompose with exposure to natural bacteria and organisms. However, it still takes at least six months to break down to 90 percent H_2O and CO_2 (American Society for Testing and Materials). Due to this, no soap should ever be used directly in a water source, and even eco-friendly soaps can contaminate water sources, harm aquatic animals, and disrupt ecosystems. This happens through the buildup of any detergent-based phosphorus leading to algae growth, leading to a reduction in oxygen necessary to maintain a healthy ecosystem (Erickson et al., 2014). Aquatic plants do need phosphorus to grow and thrive, but it is possible to have too much of a good thing. Plus, the phosphorus found in soaps is refined and often concentrated, making it more difficult for even large bodies of water to dilute properly. This is more widely seen as an issue surrounding industrial agriculture and field runoff of phosphorus-based fertilizers and manure, causing aquatic dead zones, but is still relevant to soap.

It is perfectly fine to have products that you use specifically for backpacking or camping that you may not use every day. One of those differences may even be the type of toothpaste you use. The reason I mention this is because you'll notice on the chart below that fluoride is listed on the "ingredients to avoid" in the toothpaste column. Now, I am not a dentist, so I will never advise against the use of fluoride in oral care. Still, I will advise against using fluoride toothpaste when in the backcountry to minimize environmental impact and exposure to wildlife. Fluoride can pose risks especially to aquatic organisms and sensitive plant species. You may not think that your little dab of toothpaste matters, but you are not the only person that has or will ever brush your teeth there. Over time, it adds up, and as outdoor recreation gains more and more popularity each year, it will continue to be an issue.

Sunscreens are a bit more complicated because of how they are applied and their strength. I recommend wearing sunscreen for your skin health, but you can also protect your skin with UV clothing and hats. If you choose to wear sunscreen, you can look for the "reef safe" or "reef-friendly" labeling to avoid any of the toxic ingredients listed in the chart on page 127. "Reef safe" sunscreen is a relatively new idea and that labeling is not yet regulated; most companies that use it likely have good intentions, but research company practices and ingredients. You can also look for the "protect land and sea certified" label. All of the ingredients you should avoid in sunscreens can harm coral reefs and other ecosystems and wildlife, which is the primary reason to avoid them (collectively known as the HEL list). There is not yet conclusive evidence to say how they impact human health, but they are bad for the environment regardless. Even if you are not using these sunscreens near the ocean, if you are swimming or washing any part of your body in the wilderness, these ingredients in sunscreens can be detrimental to the immediate ecosystem (Haereticus Environmental Laboratory, 2018).

There aren't a lot of questions when it comes to whether or not DEET—found in many bug repellents—may impact human health. It is a chemical, and there are warnings listed for a reason on DEET bug sprays. However, we are going to focus on the environmental impact of DEET here. Some readers may notice that in the chart on page 127, I did not include DEET on the ingredient list for bug repellent at all. (DEET can also be listed on labels as N, N-Diethyl-m-toluamide or N, N-Diethyl-3-Methyl benzamide.) That was intentional because I do see the value in DEET-free bug repellent, and it may even be necessary at times. According to the US Environmental Protection Agency (EPA), because we apply DEET bug repellents to our skin or clothes, the impact on that environment is minimal. However, it is listed as "slightly toxic" (Toxicity Category III) to birds, fish, and other aquatic animals and invertebrates, but essentially nontoxic to mammals (EPA, 1998). This toxicity report was initially published in 1998 and was most recently rereviewed in 2014.

Despite this toxicity category, a US Geological Survey listed DEET as a frequent contaminant found in streams and groundwater (Erickson et al.). It was observed that because DEET takes so long to break down in the soil, it can easily contaminate groundwater over time and with enough accumulation. The toxicity of DEET to both humans and the environment is also associated with the concentration within the bug spray, which is why Canada banned concentrations of 30 percent or higher and suggests using concentrations of 10 percent or lower.

The World Health Organization has also deemed bug sprays that contain DEET as safe and endorses them as the most effective and longest-lasting bug spray option. Still, they do not dispute that DEET can be irritating to people with sensitive skin and children. Some experts may recommend using bug repellents that use the active ingredient of picaridin instead of DEET, but it also has a high likelihood of irritating the skin and should be applied to clothing instead. Both DEET and picaridin are synthetic chemicals, meaning that they have a higher chance of being toxic to natural environments and should be used sparingly.

It is no secret that DEET-free bug sprays do not work as well. In my experience, proper clothing coverage and the willingness to reapply natural bug repellents more often (every 1–2 hours) can be just as effective. Not using any bug spray is an option, and depending on the area you are traveling, this may be feasible. Remember that certain insects (mosquitoes and ticks) are known to carry and transmit illnesses, and bug repellent is encouraged.

Soap

Ingredients to Avoid
Parabens
Petrochemicals
Ureas
Fragrance
Sodium lauryl sulfate (SLS)
Sodium laureth sulfate (SLES)
1, 4-dioxane
Triclosan
Methylisothiazolinone
Methylchloroisothiazolinone
Cocamidopropyl betaine
Phosphate
Surfactant

Eco-Safe Ingredients
Coconut oil (or other natural oils)
Bentonite
Glycerin
Aloe vera
Potassium Hydroxide (potash/ lye)
Cocamide MEA

Toothpaste

Ingredients to Avoid
Fluoride
Sodium lauryl sulfate (SLS)
Carrageenan
Propylene glycol
Triclosan

Eco-Safe Ingredients
Diatomaceous earth
Charcoal
Coconut oil
Sodium bicarbonate (baking soda)
Herb oils
Licorice root
Bentonite clay
Xylitol

Sunscreen

Ingredients to Avoid
Oxybenzone
Octinoxate
Nano titanium dioxide
Nano zinc oxide
Butylparaben
4-methylbenzylidene camphor (4MBC)
Parabens
Triclosan
Para-aminobenzoic acid (PABA)
Microplastic beads

Eco-Safe Ingredients
Non-nano zinc oxide (mineral zinc oxide)
USDA organic plant oils
Vitamin E
Beeswax
Aloe vera
Sodium palmate
Non-GMO sorbitan caprylate
Potassium iodide
Non-GMO glyceryl caprylate

Bug Repellent

Ingredients to Avoid
Cyfluthrin
Permethrin
Pyrethroids (most common chemical class for bug sprays and includes over 1,000 insecticides)

Eco-Safe Ingredients
Citronella
Lemongrass oil
Citrus oil
Clove oil
Thyme oil
Rosemary oil
Eucalyptus extract (menthane diol)
Castor oil
Vitamin E
look for botanical-based bug sprays

Although it may not be favorable to most readers, there are ways to keep yourself relatively clean and clean your dishes without the use of soap. Depending on the climate and area you are visiting, go for a swim to freshen up. To clean your pot after eating, you can use dirt and sand with some water to clean out the food remnants. You can also choose to omit sunscreens and bug sprays using bug- and UV-protective clothing.

Responsible product packaging

We covered the basics of product packaging in the "Get to Know Your Gear" and "Rethink Trail Food" chapters, but toiletries have a few unique considerations. Items like toothpaste and hand sanitizer (unless they're homemade) will be more difficult to find in containers that are not plastic. There are more and more toothpaste brands that are embracing a lower-waste alternative and natural ingredients. These may come in tablet form or a powder, which is perfect for backpacking because it is lightweight and compact. Plus, you can bring just enough for that specific trip and not carry any excess weight. The issue some backpackers may face with a tablet or powder toothpaste is keeping them dry. However, this is easy to do with a reusable airtight container.

As a general trend, most tablet and powder toothpastes do not include fluoride, which is an ingredient we should avoid in toothpaste when using them in the backcountry. Since you are likely only going to be gone for a few days or weeks at a time, this should not be an issue, but consult your dentist to see if they have a recommendation that suits your specific needs if this is a concern.

Due to shortages of hand sanitizer during the COVID-19 pandemic, there are many recipes for homemade hand sanitizer available. If making homemade anything isn't something you have time to invest in, the next best option is to buy items like soaps and hand sanitizer in bulk so you can minimize the packaging. Then, all you'll need is reusable containers to transfer to before you go backpacking. If plastic is an unavoidable option for you, try to find a recyclable package (see "Rethink Trail Food" for recycling reference information). Just remember that recycling should not be the regular fallback for our consumer goods due to the state of the recycling systems. If you are looking for a recyclable container, try to get aluminum or glass materials as these can be recycled indefinitely and are more durable to be reused.

Biodegradable soaps come in a variety of packaging options, and depending on how often you are backpacking or how long

Dental Hygiene Pros and Cons

Toothpaste

- **Pros:** comes in a variety of tube sizes, easy to use, easy to transport
- **Cons:** plastic packaging, nonrecyclable containers, depending on the brand has non-eco-friendly ingredients

Tooth Tablets

- **Pros:** lightweight, compact, easy to use, carry only what you need, natural ingredients, most brands come in glass containers
- **Cons:** need to be in an airtight container, will dissolve or mold if they get wet

Tooth Powder

- **Pros:** lightweight, natural ingredients, ability to carry only what you need, most brands come in glass containers
- **Cons:** can be difficult to use, often has a strange taste (clay), must be kept in an airtight container to keep dry

you are in the backcountry, which one you choose may be based more on how long it will last than whether it comes in a plastic bottle or not. As mentioned before, the ingredients you use in the soap should outweigh the packaging it comes in, especially if one bottle will last you several expeditions.

When looking at your options for biodegradable soaps, if you want to avoid plastics, your best option is almost always going to be soap sheets. Soap sheets remove the water in soap and concentrate the other ingredients into a lightweight, portable sheet. Not all soap sheet brands use compostable packaging, though. Many big-name outdoor companies use plastic containers for their soap sheets to keep them dry. This is a very logical packaging choice for that purpose, but you can easily keep soap sheets dry in a reusable container.

An example of a soap sheet company that uses compostable paper packaging is KindLather. This makes some things complicated because if soap sheets get wet, they'll dissolve. Like many of our other low-waste switches, you will need to use a reusable container to carry them. Another benefit of soap sheets is that you can easily tear off only what you will need for your trip. Instead of bringing an entire bottle of liquid soap for a weekend trip, you can simply pack 2–4 soap sheets saving space and weight, even if it is just a few ounces. They use all plant-based ingredients for their soap, and their packaging is a dissolvable paper that can be reused, recycled, or composted.

Although your first concern when you are packing for a backcountry trip might be the durability and usability of the product packaging, shift that thought process to become *what is the afterlife of this product packaging?* With more low-waste and eco-conscious companies popping up, especially within the outdoor industry, products that don't come in plastic packaging are becoming increasingly accessible.

The product materials

During this transition process, don't hyperfocus on packaging alone. Consider the entire product life cycle, including that of the packaging and its afterlife. If you need a refresher on product life cycles and the importance of understanding them, flip back to the "Get to Know Your Gear" chapter.

Soap Pros and Cons

Bar Soap

- **Pros:** affordable, generally low life cycle impact, made from fats and oil, longest-lasting, minimal packaging
- **Cons:** not very multifunctional, requires more water to use, bacteria can build up if not stored properly, harder to transport, often has a higher pH level

Liquid Soap

- **Pros:** multipurpose in the backcountry, easy to use, comes in a bottle for easy transport, long life span if stored well
- **Cons:** comes in a plastic bottle, most often contains more ingredients and chemicals, more expensive, can be hard to find fragrance free

Soap Sheets

- **Pros:** most compact option, lightweight, very versatile, easy to use, can come in compostable packaging, never expire
- **Cons:** must be stored carefully because if they get wet they'll dissolve, requires multiple sheets for washing dishes or clothes, hands must be dry to remove a sheet from the package

Disposable Wipes

- **Pros:** easy to use, no water required, easy to carry, a good option when showers and privacy are not available
- **Cons:** single-use item, plastic packaging and plastic in wipes themselves, must pack them out, bulkier to carry compared to other cleaning options

Product Materials to Look For When Choosing Backcountry Toiletries

- **Toothbrush:** Opt for bamboo instead of plastic. They last just as long as a conventional toothbrush and will decompose within 3–4 months in the right conditions.

- **Trowel:** Always get a steel trowel. Plastic is lighter, but steel is more durable and can be recycled indefinitely.

- **Pee Rag:** Bamboo fabric is naturally antibacterial, antimicrobial, and antifungal. A bandana works, but innovative pee rags exist now (check out the WanderWipe or Kula Cloth that use bamboo fabric on one side and waterproof fabric on the other side). Pee rags are meant to replace toilet paper for women after peeing in the wilderness.

- **Towel:** Avoid microfiber towels that are petroleum-based and shed plastics into the environment. Opt for natural, plant-based materials. Consider a towel from Lava Linens. Their towels are French linen derived from flax plants and as a company, they exemplify sustainable practices from the start of production to the product afterlife. Lava Linens fabric is an incredibly durable, absorbent, packable, and naturally antimicrobial towel option.

- **Menstrual Cup or Underwear:** Menstrual cups are most commonly made from medical-grade silicone, rubber, latex, or elastomer. These are meant to replace single-use menstrual items like tampons and pads and, if used properly and cleaned regularly, can last up to 10 years. Period underwear is another popular low-waste period option, and for short hikes, these can be changed and carried until the end of your trip. You can wash them as needed on longer treks. If tampons are the only option you're comfortable with, opt for tampons without an applicator and ones made from organic cotton.

- **Resealable Waterproof Bag:** Consider a reusable nursery bag like the Planet Wise Wet Bag. These are designed to hold and carry dirty diapers without leaking, meaning they are a perfect reusable option for a disposable plastic bag to carry used toilet paper, tampons, food scraps, and other wet items. Plus, they're machine washable.

PROPER WASTE DISPOSAL IN THE BACKCOUNTRY

Waste goes beyond the trash from food wrappers, especially on a multiday trip. Waste will include human waste, food waste, toothpaste, and soapy water from doing dishes or bathing. Proper pet waste disposal is covered in the "Pet Problems" chapter. In this section, we'll build on Principle 3 of the Leave No Trace Guidelines—Dispose of Waste Properly—and discuss things to keep in mind when disposing of waste in the backcountry.

Wastewater and toothpaste

How you use toiletries in the wilderness is just as important as the ingredients you choose. First, avoid bathing in streams, lakes, or any other water source using soap of any kind. You can go swimming and rinse your body in those water sources, but soap should not be used. Leave No Trace guidelines suggest that when bathing or washing dishes in the wilderness, collect water and take it at least 200 feet away from any water source. Washes (dry intermittent stream channels and water drainages) are also water sources, so you should not bathe in a wash or near a wash of any kind. Avoiding washes is important because they lead to larger bodies of water, so after it rains, any waste that collects in a wash is effectively carried to the nearest water source.

Use soap sparingly and when you are ready to dispose of wastewater, dig a hole at least 6–8 inches deep to bury the water. Using this cathole method assists the breakdown of the soap residue and minimizes the scent for wildlife. If you are bathing outdoors, dig this hole ahead of time and hang a water bladder above the hole. Then, you can wash dishes, hands, or hair above the hole, and the water will collect. If this is not an option, then collect wastewater in a bucket or basin of some kind and dispose of it after you're finished.

There are several options for toothpaste disposal that will leave little to no trace. First, you can swallow it. This is not advised if you are backpacking for extended periods. Swallowing natural toothpaste a couple of times a day on a weekend trip isn't going to harm a healthy adult, but children should avoid it. If this does not work for you, choose to spit the toothpaste in the firepit (if you're using it). That way, the toothpaste will not be interacting with the environment around camp and will be burned up the next time the firepit is used. The best recommendation is to have a camp "sump" or a 6- to 8-inch-deep hole for you to use to spit toothpaste into just as you use to dispose of your wastewater.

Things like wastewater and toothpaste don't always feel like a big deal. After all, you're just one group or one person: How much could one day's worth of toothpaste damage that environment? But we are not the only ones using those areas. Most hiking areas have designated campsites, so although you may not see anyone else on your camping trip, rest assured that hundreds, maybe even thousands of other people will use that exact same area. Over time, the buildup of soapy wastewater and toothpaste will damage that area's ecosystem.

Food waste

Do your best to avoid having or leaving food waste in the wilderness. Have self-awareness regarding how much you will eat during a meal to avoid having to carry out or dispose of food waste while camping or backpacking. This is not always possible, as sometimes heat, exhaustion, and other factors can influence our appetite. Not to mention when camping with kids, they're more likely not to finish snacks or meals. Whatever the case might be, food waste either needs to be packed out in a wet bag or buried in a 6- to 8-inch-deep hole.

Food waste doesn't usually cause too much of an ecological hazard, depending on the food and climate, but it does pose a threat to wildlife in the area. Much like tossing an apple core or a banana peel, anytime excess food is left at a campsite, it draws in various wild animals. If this becomes a frequent occurrence, animals will begin to visit the camping areas more often, potentially posing a threat to their own safety as well as visitors.

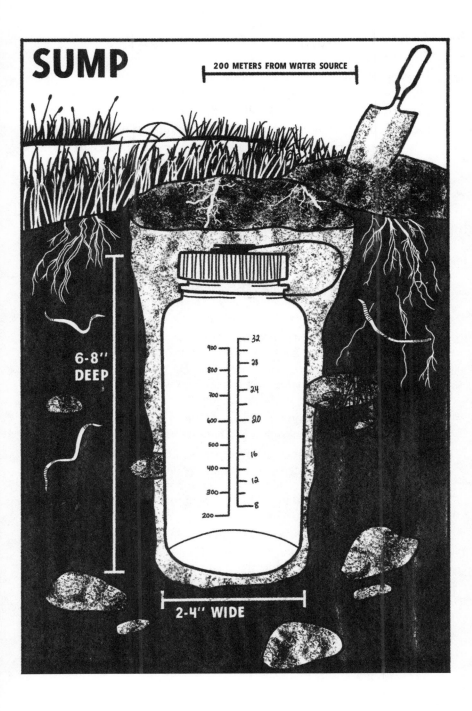

Human waste

Depending on the type of camping you are participating in, you may have to poop in the woods. Some designated camping areas have pit toilets (latrine that collects human waste in a hole in the ground), which help minimize the issue of human waste. Still, as you venture farther into the backcountry, you will need to dispose of human waste yourself. To do this properly, you have two choices: dig a cathole to bury it or carry it out in a wag bag.

How to Dig and Use a Cathole

- Find a location at least 200 feet away from the nearest water source and wash. Be sure this is a place where you will be capable of digging a hole of the appropriate size (avoid roots and rocky areas).

- Dig your hole using your camping trowel. If you do not have a trowel, find a sturdy stick or use a rock. This will take longer, but it is doable. Be sure the hole is 4 to 6 inches wide and 6 to 8 inches deep (tip: use a Nalgene bottle to gauge the depth).

- Once your cathole is prepped, find a sturdy straddling position and poop into the hole.

- Do not bury wipes or toilet paper in the cathole (unless using camping-specific biodegradable toilet paper). All other toilet paper or wipes must be packed out with you, along with any menstrual items like tampons or pads.

- Once you're finished with your business, cover the cathole. You should mound the hole with the dirt to be sure that it has the best chance of breaking down properly, and so when it rains, the hole does not sink in on itself. You can also add some leaves or other organic materials on top of the hole to help the decomposition process.

It's not always a choice—some backcountry areas do not allow catholes, meaning all human waste must be carried out. The cathole method is much like disposing of other types of waste—you'll dig a 4- to 6-inch-wide, 6- to 8-inch-deep hole and bury waste inside it. If your cathole is not deep or wide enough, it will take longer for your waste to break down in that environment.

Wag bags are the other option available for dealing with human waste in the backcountry. These are also known as go anywhere toilet kits or travel toilet bags. These bags are specially designed to carry and dispose of human waste during expeditions, making them durable and reducing any risk of leakage or smell. Most wag bags are made to be puncture-resistant, contain a small hand sanitizer packet or alcohol wipe, poo powder to mask the odor, and a small amount of toilet paper. While these are very useful, they all must be disposed of in the trash after use. They cannot be flushed or put in a pit toilet of any kind.

How to Use a Wag Bag

- Take the bag liner out of the outer, puncture-resistant bag.
- Remove toilet paper and hand sanitizer/alcohol pad.
- Get into a stable squatting position.
- Hold the bag below your hips in a way that allows you to capture your waste.
- If it wasn't already loose inside the inner bag, add the poo powder once you've wiped.
- Sanitize and add other waste items like trash into the bag.
- Cinch the loop to seal the inner pouch completely.
- Put the inner pouch inside the outer puncture-proof bag, and seal.

BACKPACKING WITH BABIES

Many parents bring their children on various outdoor adventures ranging in difficulty. It isn't uncommon for parents to pack an infant with them on a backpacking trip. Taking your baby with you into the wilderness does require more planning and precaution than it does when you're on your own, but it can be done safely with the right considerations and gear. While I am not here to instruct you on how to safely bring your child outdoors, we do need to talk about backpacking with babies and what to do with their diapers.

Most low-waste families that bring an infant trekking choose to use reusable cloth diapers. This will be a similar experience to using menstrual underwear. On a short trek, you may be able to get by packing a wet bag and storing used diapers after changing. However, for longer hikes, only packing four or five diapers and washing them as you go is a better option. When washing diapers, removing fecal matter and disposing of it in the same way you dispose of your waste is recommended, along with the wastewater produced when washing the diapers. Follow Leave No Trace guidelines for washing clothes 200 feet away from water sources when washing diapers and never wash dirty diapers in water sources.

Baby wipes are another commonly discussed item within the zero-waste communities, and honestly, they are a super convenient way to keep not only yourself but your baby clean when in the backcountry. You can choose to use wipes in these situations, but you need to pack out waste after you use them. A better alternative is a reusable cloth that you clean with biodegradable soap after each use. That way, you only have to pack one, and while it may take longer to wash it each time, it eliminates the need for carrying out or producing additional waste.

Still, it doesn't make you a bad parent if you wait until your child is out of diapers before bringing them! Do what is right for your situation, but know that there are options available if you choose them.

WHAT ABOUT YOUR FIRST-AID KIT ITEMS?

In writing this book, I ended up reading a lot of zero-waste content just to see what was out there in comparison to my experiences. In a few of the sustainable and zero-waste outdoor spaces online, I noticed recommendations for zero-waste first-aid kits. Unfortunately, some of these recommendations omitted necessary first-aid items like antiseptics and replaced them with more natural options like manuka honey. Here's the thing: Yes, manuka honey is a natural antiseptic. However, I do not believe that when we venture into the backcountry that we should risk our health to achieve the goal of being zero-waste.

Being low-waste is not a black-and-white issue. There is a lot of gray area, and for the outdoor minimalist, the first-aid kit is going to be a gray area. Most medical items in a first-aid kit have waste associated with them, and that may be something we have to accept until the industry comes up with better sterile, safe solutions.

Don't eliminate or skimp out on first-aid kit items on a camping or backpacking trip simply because they create waste. Your safety in the outdoors is also important and avoiding things like infections when on an expedition is a part of that safety piece.

You can buy first-aid kits that include most of these items, or you can create your own to further customize it for your needs. The list above is what I recommend specifically for backcountry trips, especially if access to medical attention may be days away. For car camping trips or RVing, a less-extensive first-aid kit is likely to be just fine depending on the remoteness of your location.

Backcountry First-Aid Kit Items

☐ A variety of gauze pads (different sizes)
☐ Blister treatment
☐ Nonstick sterile pads
☐ Medical tape
☐ Butterfly tape/wound closure strips
☐ Compound tincture of benzoin
☐ Adhesive bandages
☐ Other wound care products (elastic wrap, liquid bandage, hemostatic gauze, rolled gauze, SAM splint, finger splint, triangular cravat bandage)
☐ Antibiotic ointment
☐ Antiseptic wipes
☐ Pain relief medications (ibuprofen, aspirin)
☐ Antihistamine
☐ Diarrhea medication
☐ Oral rehydration salts
☐ Prescription medications
☐ Insect sting treatment
☐ Throat lozenges
☐ Burn treatment
☐ Cotton swabs
☐ Tweezers
☐ Safety pins
☐ Thermometer
☐ Emergency blanket
☐ Blunt-tip scissors
☐ Safety razor blade
☐ Surgical gloves
☐ Irrigation syringe with 18-gauge catheter
☐ CPR mask
☐ If needed: Epipen, glucose
☐ Recommended: small notepad, pen, first-aid manual

Cheat Sheet: Product Priorities

If you are struggling to identify quality products, whether it be general gear or toiletries, refer back to the "Get to Know Your Gear" chapter.

You can also use this list of product priority considerations as a quick way to identify quality options and narrow down your choices:

- Inputs to and types of raw materials
- Versatility of the item
- Life span of product
- End-of-life or afterlife of product
- Product packaging, shipping materials, and promotional materials used
- Other forms of sustainability in terms of worker safety and wages

*Product priorities checklist developed in collaboration with Mary Swanson of Lava Linens.

Pet Problems

Let me get this out of the way before you even start reading this chapter: I have a dog, and I love him dearly. Ash is my favorite adventure partner, and he honestly comes with me everywhere (that he is allowed).

If you're reading this chapter, I'm guessing you have a pet of some kind, most likely a dog. Many outdoor enthusiasts have an adventure pup! Whatever type of pet you have, there are so many benefits to their company, and they add so much texture to our daily lives. They become a part of the family, and as we begin to treat our pets like our children, we strive to give them the best life possible. This may come in the form of optimal nutrition, the best toys, or even proper gear so they can enjoy the outdoors with you as the seasons change. Much like humans, pets do have an impact on the environment simply by existing. I'm not advocating for anyone to get rid of their pet. I am saying, though, that as we start to evaluate our environmental impact with more depth, we should also begin to assess the impact our pets have on the environment to make future decisions accordingly.

Pets add an extra layer of consideration to outdoor minimalist practices. In this chapter, I will outline some of the general environmental implications of having a pet, and then I will break down how we can minimize their impact when we bring them hiking and camping.

GENERAL IMPACT OF PETS ON THE ENVIRONMENT

Before diving right into outdoor minimalism with pets, you first need to understand how they make an impact. Awareness is often the precursor to action, so much like us learning about the human implications of outdoor recreation on the environment, we need to get to know how our pets fit into that picture.

Pets make an impact on the outdoors via three main categories: food, gear, and waste. Breeding does impact the environment, and I do encourage you to adopt instead of buying. For the purposes of this guide, though, we'll focus on what you can control going forward.

Food

As discussed in the "Rethink Trail Food" chapter, the food we eat has serious consequences for the environment. The same can be said for the food our pets eat, except they can't shift to a plant-based diet as easily as we can. Cats and dogs eat heavily meat-based foods produced by industrial agriculture, which has a massive environmental impact. A large portion of pet food is made from byproducts of animals slaughtered for human consumption. Animal byproducts are essentially the body parts of animals that are not suitable for humans, particularly the leftover carcasses, organs, and other animal parts most people would never look at, let alone eat.

Some readers may see this as a positive use of these slaughtered animals because then nothing is going to waste. However, it is problematic for the health of our pets, as many of these animal parts come from livestock that were raised on factory farms and are pumped with antibiotics and likely riddled with cancers. While most cancerous tumors are removed from human-grade meat, they are often ground up and combined with other animal byproducts to be fed to our pets (Winters, 2020). While it may not be the healthiest option for our pets or the planet, the pet food industry is a big one. According to the USDA's meat price spreads, livestock byproducts make up anywhere from 4 to 15 percent of the total value of the animal, depending on the type of animal and the given year (USDA, 2021). Economically, it wouldn't make sense to remove animal byproducts from pet food, because it is in demand and pet food companies are willing to pay for it. Pet food is not the only industrial use for animal byproducts, but it is a large percentage. In many ways, the way our pet food is made is tied back to our diets, because the more animals produced and slaughtered for human consumption, the more byproducts are available to sell for pet food.

As this information has become more mainstream, there has been a rise in interest in pet food quality. Many pet owners are paying more attention to what they are feeding their pets, but cats and dogs are likely still eating meat. Cats are obligate carnivores and need meat to survive. Domesticated dogs can survive on plants because they are omnivores due to their scavenging nature (Bosch, Plantinga, and Hendriks, 2014). Keep in mind that any significant diet changes you make with your pet should be done under the guidance of a veterinarian and pet health expert because, much like humans, our pets have food sensitivities, allergies, and specific dietary needs.

As more pet owners switch to food options made with human-grade animal products instead of animal byproducts, we begin to see how their meat consumption has an environmental impact outside of the meat humans eat. A study published in 2017 concluded that cats and dogs in the United States make up 25–30 percent of the environmental impacts of animal agriculture through their diet. This percentage range was calculated considering the use of land, water, fossil fuels, phosphates, and biocides used during agricultural production. Americans have the largest number of companion animals of any country in the world. Other countries like China are beginning to buy into the pet industry more, which further increases the demand to feed our cats and dogs (Okin, 2017).

The major hurdle with pet food, particularly for cats, is that they don't have the same dietary flexibility as humans. So the only way to truly address the impact of the pet food industry is to decrease the number of pets we have to feed and overhaul how we produce pet food.

Looking at our pet obsession objectively and evaluating the necessity of pets in our lives is important. That doesn't mean caring for your pets any less. If you are already a pet owner, you can reduce the impact your beloved pet has on the environment. Start by looking at their diet from a health and sustainability standpoint. Get to know common ingredients, where food comes from, and how it is processed.

Start to read pet food labels and look for identifiable ingredients. Much like with human food, transparency is key. The extent to which pet food is processed can obscure actual ingredients and their origins. Look for companies that are listing the actual foods used to create the dried food pellets such as rice, turkey, carrots, and sweet potatoes. When labels list any meat meal or byproduct on the label, you know that they are not using human-grade meat ingredients. Pet foods labeled as dinners, entrees, or nuggets typically only contain about 25 percent meat content. Meals that say they have meat "flavorings" or "with [meat type]" will typically only contain trace amounts of meat content.

The Food and Drug Administration (FDA) does regulate pet food to an extent, but unfortunately the FDA doesn't always enforce regulations in the pet food industry. They conduct relatively infrequent inspection of pet food manufacturing facilities and ingredient suppliers, except for USDA-regulated suppliers. They will also conduct investigations if there is a complaint filed by a consumer or veterinarian. Where the pet food is manufactured also plays a role in the regulations because the FDA works with the AAFCO (Association of American Feed Control Offices) to develop state laws, define ingredients, and establish nutritional requirements. Lastly, the FDA is also responsible for approving or denying additives or processing aids (GRAS or Generally Recognized as Safe ingredients). So many irregularities exist within the regulation of pet food quality, because these FDA processes are not guided by federal law.

Although the USDA does not have authority over pet food regulations and requirements, they do have a voluntary pet food certification program. This program isn't recognized by the State Department of Agriculture or the FDA but is the same structure as the USDA's regulation for human-grade meat under their FSIS (Food and Safety Inspection) division. When human-grade meat meant for pet food is raw, the USDA inspects it, but once it is manufactured into pet food, the USDA no longer has jurisdiction. At this point, APHIS (Animal Plant Health Inspection Services) may provide limited oversight as a division of the USDA.

While there are a lot of hands in the bucket of pet food, the major authority in regulation is the FDA. They have written some compliance policies, but they are loose and can feel kind of illegal if you read into them. As an example, one of the compliance policies that is surprising is that "pet food consisting of material from diseased animals or animals which have died otherwise than by slaughter, which is a violation of 402(a)(5) will not ordinarily be actionable, if it is not otherwise in violation of the law. It will be considered fit for animal consumption."

Pet food is seemingly not well regulated, and the regulations that do exist are confusing and hard for even those in charge of inspections and quality management to follow and enforce. While human-grade meat is often better regulated for quality, both pet and human food product labels are not all regulated. For instance, the word *natural* is not a regulated term in the pet food industry, but *organic* is. Awareness of which words are backed up by a third-party certification is helpful to make more informed decisions.

Then there's the question of what those ingredients are wrapped in: pet food packaging. It is possible to buy pet food in bulk using your own reusable containers, but it is rare. Most of the time, we are buying our pet food in a bag of some kind. These bags are often made of paper, but many pet food companies have begun to switch to thick resealable plastic bags to preserve the freshness of food. In theory, this makes a lot of sense for customer convenience, but it doesn't make sense for the afterlife of that packaging. Most pet owners buy pet food once a month in a size that makes sense for their pet. On top of that, pet owners are also buying several treats and supplements that come in plastic packaging. Most wet food, which is more commonly fed to cats than dogs, comes in a can, making it easy to recycle. Still, most of the time, one can is only enough for one meal for that animal. Some of our pets eat two to three times per day, and all of that food, processing, and waste adds up throughout their life.

Small herbivorous pets, like rabbits, tend to have less of an impact on the planet simply because they do not eat farmed animals. Wild animals are a different story, but domesticated animals primarily eat food that humans grow, process, and provide for them to eat.

Gear

The pet industry produces a ton of waste aside from food, from household toys to silly outfits. For the outdoor minimalist, let's focus on gear you may use with a pet when you go on an outdoor adventure. Many of these things will overlap with other aspects of pet gear and equipment, so you can also apply them to other areas of your life with your pet.

I can't speak for everyone that is a pet owner, but I can speak from my own experience with my dog. In recent years, I have spent an uncomfortable amount of time researching and looking into outdoor gear for him. We went to pet stores to try on harnesses and life jackets, and yes, he has a full snow getup, boots and all. I wanted him to be able to come with me no matter the weather conditions, and I needed him to have the right gear so he could be safe and comfortable the entire time. If you own an outdoor adventure dog or even a hunting dog, you might also have an embarrassingly large bin of dog gear, not including their general toys and bones to enjoy when you're at home.

We are not alone in this pursuit with our pets. The American Pet Products Association (APPA) reported that in 2020 the pet industry reached record sales with $103.6 billion. That is almost a 7 percent increase in sales of pet products over the previous year. Around $22 billion of that was spent on pet supplies. The dramatic increase of pet adoptions throughout the COVID-19 pandemic certainly contributed to the massive rise in pet spending. Regardless of global circumstances, our willingness to have pets and provide them with products that make their lives with us happier and healthier continues to grow.

When we are looking at outdoor pet gear, we want to look at it through the same minimalist mindset we are applying to consumer goods we buy for ourselves. Several outdoor brands make pet-specific products, usually for dogs, but one of the primary considerations outside of the product life cycle pet owners need to focus on is the product's durability. When I'm thinking about some of the places and adventures that my dog and I have enjoyed, I also think about the number of jackets or hiking vests he has effectively destroyed simply by wearing them outside. Most of these were early on in my ownership and before I started to take the whole product life cycle and durability into consideration when buying. My main focus when first purchasing outdoor gear for him was affordability. After all, I was already spending enough money on gear for me, and now I had to shell out even more to bring him along.

I found myself spending too much money on frequently replacing low-quality dog gear because the high-quality equipment seemed out of my budget. Then a friend shared an old saying that changed my perspective: "It is expensive to be poor." If you're on a tight budget or living paycheck to paycheck, you can't always make the best long-term financial choices. If you only have $5 to spend on a dog jacket, you'll be spending $5 on a new dog jacket every couple of months. If you're able to spend $80+ on a higher-quality jacket, it will likely last the life span of your dog.

Most of the research into the environmental impact of pets is hyperfocused on food and waste. These are important, but they are not the only part of pet ownership that impacts the environment. Think about walking into a pet superstore like PetSmart or Petco. What do you see? Usually, an overwhelming amount of cheap toys, copious amounts of treats, pet beds, and even clothes for our pets. Most of this is completely unnecessary to the happiness and health of our pets, yet there is a market for it largely because of our exposure to consumer culture. Much like we want the best for our kids or ourselves, we want the best and the newest for our pets. The funny thing is that my dog could care less about how he looks in his snow jacket. He's simply happy being outside, playing in the snow with me.

As you are starting to evaluate your own needs regarding outdoor gear and equipment, start to do the same for your pet's gear. Do they need six more squeaky toys they're going to destroy in a matter of minutes? Once you identify their practical needs, you can start looking at some of the other aspects of choosing pet gear like price, quality, and sustainability, much like you do for your own gear. When it comes to pet gear, we need to start shopping outside the focus of cuteness and more within the realm of practicality and application.

Waste

Have you ever noticed how within the first 200 feet or so of any hiking trail that allows dogs, there seems to be an absurd number of dog poop bags? Or worse, piles of unbagged dog poop and that gnarly smell you know was only created by all the dogs peeing on another dog's pee. Most dogs will end up pooping within the first 200 feet of a hiking trail because of the excitement and the overwhelming smell of the other dogs that have passed through the area. The hope is that all dog owners are responsible enough to clean up after their pet, but unfortunately, this is not the case. The ones that do bag their dog's poop don't always make it to the trash

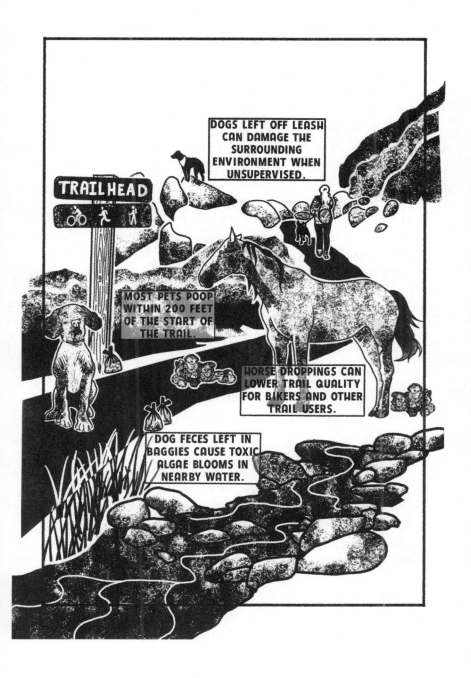

either. That's why we see bags of poop that are piled up together under signposts, tossed to the side of the trail, or my personal favorite, hanging from a tree. Most dog owners that do this are well-intentioned. They just don't want to carry the dog poop bag for the entire hike, so they plan to grab it on the way out.

The thing is, if you forget to pick it up and toss it on your way out, it sits there until someone from the park or a trail cleanup crew comes through and picks it up. I get it. I've been there. I vividly remember an incident in Moab, Utah, when my dog and I had hiked a beautiful desert trail, got back to the car, and I realized I forgot to pick up the poop I had bagged over a mile into our hike. I even remembered the specific rock I set it on underneath a juniper tree because I didn't want it roasting in the sun. I didn't want to go back, but I couldn't bear the thought of leaving it there. I couldn't be *that* person! I decided to run back the 1 mile and collect the dog poop, but what if I hadn't remembered or taken the time to go back and get it? Unless someone else had come through the area and picked up the bag, that bag of dog poop would take years to degrade, and what was left would potentially harm wildlife and release toxins into the ecosystem. I think of that incident often when I'm hiking, and it inspires me to pick up trash and other people's dog poop on hikes. This is a great habit to get into. Bring an extra bag and pick up a few pieces of trash or even one extra dog poop on your way out to help keep the trail clean.

Pet waste poses many issues both on and off hiking trails. It is estimated that at least 67 percent of American households, or 84.9 million homes own pets (APPA, 2020). All of those animals poop. The most commonly discussed pet poop in terms of environmental impact is often dog poop, but we must also remember that all of our other pets also poop. For instance, when we dispose of cat poop, we often dispose of kitty litter, and many cat owners bag their cat poop and litter combo in a plastic bag. The 2020 APPA survey also found that there are now around 77 million dogs living in the United States. It is also estimated that, on average, dogs produce ¾ of a pound of waste each day. This is an average because breeds and dog size impact how much poop is produced each day (i.e., a chihuahua will poop far less than a mastiff). If that's true, then dogs alone are producing around 10 million pounds of poop each year.

Pet waste has become an increasingly important environmental issue, because there are not very effective waste management systems in place. As humans, our waste is usually managed in a way that keeps our communities safe and clean. Our pets, dogs specifically, poop outside, and it is then our responsibility to scoop it up and find a way to dispose of it. The go-to disposal method of our pet poop is to pick it up and put it in the trash to be sent to the landfill. If you are gathering dog poop in your yard, you may use a poop scoop and a bucket to dump it into your trash. If you are on a walk in the neighborhood or a hike, you will most likely pick up the poop in a plastic poop bag. Then, hopefully, you carry that poop bag to the nearest trash bin or dog poop collection bin. Many hiking trails and dog parks will provide pet poop stations to make it easy and accessible for dog owners to pick up the poop, but most stations only provide poop bags. I have been to some dog parks in Arizona that provide a rake and shovel instead of bags, which works quite well because the ground is sandy in those parks.

Before we talk about the impact of how we pick up dog poop, we need to also look at why it is essential to clean it up. There have been several instances when I'm hiking with someone new, and I have my dog along. Eventually, I have to stop and pick up his poop. Some of them continue the conversation we were having, but a handful of people stop me to say, "leave it! You wouldn't pick up a coyote's poop. What's the difference?" Honestly, I encourage these questions because it opens up a dialogue with them to explain the environmental dangers and impact of dog poop. Much like the misconception that since an apple core or a banana peel is organic waste, it is okay to throw on the trail, just because dog poop is natural does not make it safe to leave anywhere.

The first issue with leaving dog poop is that it is gross, and the sheer number of dogs that exist would mean that if no one ever picked up their dog poop, we would eventually have piles and piles of dog poop on hiking trails. That poop would eventually break down some and mash down onto the soil. This may not seem like a big deal, but dog poop contains a dense amount of bacteria and parasites that contaminate ecosystems and spread disease to wild animals, other dogs, and even humans. Both the CDC and the EPA have resources on their websites that explain that just 1 gram of dog poop contains up to 23 million fecal coliform bacteria. Not only that, but dog poop has commonly been found to carry hookworms, roundworms, whipworms, giardia, salmonella, E. coli, parvo, coronavirus strains, cryptosporidium, and campylobacter (Cinquepalmi et al., 2013). Cat poop poses other human disease concerns but is less frequently left in wild spaces, making exposure far less frequent for people other than the owners. However, stray and outdoor cats may pose more of an environmental risk.

The main argument I hear from most hikers that leave dog poop is that wild animals poop in the woods, so it is okay. However, part of why dog poop contains all of these different bacteria and parasites is because of the food they eat. A wild animal is eating food that comes directly from that ecosystem. That's not to say that their poop doesn't contain bacteria of any kind, but it isn't foreign to the ecosystem. Dog food is nutrient-dense, which is why we feed it to our pets, but it also contains high levels of nitrogen and phosphorus by the time it comes out in the form of poop. If you are a gardener or farmer, you may know that nitrogen and phosphorus are common nutrients found in fertilizers. That may lead you to believe that dog poop would be good for the environment, but as we learned in the toiletries chapter, you can have too much of a good thing. When it rains, leftover dog poop will start to break down, and these nutrients will disperse, often running off into the nearest water source leading to an imbalance of nutrients in that ecosystem. High levels of nitrogen and phosphorus can lead to algae blooms that encourage the growth of invasive plant species and can also suffocate aquatic ecosystems by using up too much oxygen. Gradually, these subtle changes can have a dramatic and detrimental impact on an entire ecosystem (Stevens and Hussmann, 2017).

Pet waste is not only an issue on hiking trails, though. It also can cause problems within towns, parks, and sewage systems. Many pet owners that have yards may even leave their pet's poop in the yard to break down naturally over time. If they aren't using the yard regularly, this does not seem like an issue to them, but that same spread of bacteria washes into storm drains and nearby water sources every time it rains.

Obviously, everyone should pick up their dog's poop, but that's not a total fix. The sheer amount of pet waste that goes to the landfill each year is also an issue. While tossing waste away in plastic bags removes the pet waste from the immediate environment and prevents the spread of bacteria and parasites, it doesn't eliminate the impact of that waste completely. Much like other organic waste like food scraps, a landfill does not provide the proper environment for pet waste to effectively break down. Pet waste releases methane into the atmosphere as it decomposes—that is if it breaks down at all. Since such a large percentage of pet waste is disposed of in nonbiodegradable plastic bags, that waste could essentially become "mummified" in the landfill until the bag is ripped or degrades enough to expose the poop. All of this further adds to the extensive amount of plastic waste already in existence. Even pet waste bags labeled as biodegradable or compostable will not fully break down or take years to break down into smaller pieces when sent to the landfill because they are intended to be processed in industrial composting facilities.

The good news is that several large municipalities are well aware of the impact that dog poop has on their waste system, and they are working on coming up with solutions. The most common implementation is composting dog poop bags in an industrial manner to be used as fertilizer for nonedible plants like trees or other city landscaping. Another solution that has begun to gain traction is a dog waste digester invented by Matthew Mazzotta used to power lights in one Cambridge dog park in England. Much like other biodigesters models, since the dog poop creates methane as it decomposes, the mechanism can convert the methane produced by composting dog poop into electricity to power the lights when functioning correctly.

There are a few other options to deal with dog poop if you do not live in a city with a dedicated industrial composting facility. Some cities allow you to flush dog waste (not cat waste), but not in a bag. This is very specific to the waste system and the department of sanitation regulations for the city. If you're considering flushing pet waste, look into this for your city first as it can cause complications in plumbing systems. Other options are to bury the waste in your yard at least a foot deep and below a runoff zone. If you decide to bury pet waste, be sure to keep it far away from any edible plants you may be growing to prevent the spread of zoonotic diseases. You can also invest in pet waste–specific composting systems for your home and apply the completed compost to nonedible plants.

Whatever the solution you choose, there is one common factor: You need to pick up the pet waste. If even compostable poop bags aren't all that environmentally friendly, what is the next best option? If you are in your yard, you can easily get a poop scoop and a bucket to pick up your dog's poop. If you are on a walk, at the dog park, or on a hike, one of the only nonplastic alternatives is to use a product like Pooch Paper. Pooch Paper is made from recycled, unbleached paper with a wax-like coating, similar to paper sandwich wrapping, to make it safe and sanitary to pick up and carry dog poop. These are best used when they can also be deposited in composting, because when sent to the landfill, the decomposition of the poop will still release methane. However, it makes it less impactful because the waste no longer is being "mummified" within the plastic bag and isn't contributing to plastic pollution.

Dangers to Pets When Hiking and Camping

Even though our dogs and cats seemingly thrive on the trail or when out camping, that doesn't mean there are no risks involved. First have reliable training and knowledge of your pet's limits. Then consider other safety precautions such as appropriate vaccinations and awareness of the environment. Some of the most common dangers our pets face when we take them out on the trail with us include:

- **Wildlife:** For small dogs, larger predators like coyotes present a threat. In certain areas, pack hunters like javelinas can threaten a dog of any size. Other animals such as venomous snakes and even prey that may be carrying disease all pose risks. We recommend doing your best to keep your pet in sight at all times. Even in off-leash areas, dogs should be under control and have reliable recall. Before venturing out, dogs should also be treated for fleas, ticks, and heartworm.

- **Weather:** Whether it is too hot or too cold, know your pet's needs and their limits. Many dogs suffer from heat exhaustion or heatstroke when hiking in temperatures too hot for their bodies. Other dangers include burning their paws on sand or pavement. Not all dogs are built for the cold, so they should be provided the appropriate gear. Even snow dogs that thrive in cold temperatures can still suffer from chapped paws and should use protective boots or balm.

- **Allergies:** All animals can have allergies. You can get them tested before you go and pay close attention to them when outside. Common outdoor allergens can include pollen, grass, and other plants.

(continued)

Dangers to Pets When Hiking and Camping (*continued*)

- **Toxins:** Be aware of your pet's location at all times. You want to prevent them from eating things, chasing wildlife, digging, and drinking water from certain sources. In some areas, like Arizona, bacteria in the dirt can cause illness, and digging should be prevented. Provide safe drinking water for your dog to avoid exposure to toxic algae that may be present. Always research water contamination and sources before traveling into the backcountry. Dogs can become ill or even die from simply swimming in water containing toxic algae. The best practice is to provide dogs with treated water.

- **Trail Conditions:** Plants, rocks, sticks, and more can all be hazardous to your pet. Have them wear boots if there are a lot of spiky plants. Ensure they stay on the trail or keep them on a leash to prevent them from getting injured. Carry a pet first-aid kit to treat common injuries such as paw abrasions.

- **Other People:** Not all people are dog people, so keep your dog under control at all times. Prevent them from rushing up to others to avoid a confrontation. Train your dog and familiarize them with bikes and horses to ensure they won't chase or react when hiking. If you're unsure how they will respond to new stimuli, keep your dog on a leash.

- **Other Dogs:** Knowing your dog's limits and training is great, but you'll never know about other dogs. Many dogs enjoy being off-leash, but not all have reliable recall. Be prepared if a dog rushes up to your dog and contain the interaction to the best of your ability. Always advocate for your dog and your space.

Low-Waste Tips for Camping and Hiking with Pets

Although you can easily apply some of the information I provided earlier to your daily life and even your outdoor adventures with your pet, here are some more specific things you can do to help minimize your pet's impact when you go hiking, backpacking, or camping with them. I have broken this section into four distinct categories: dogs, cats, horses (and pack animals like llamas), and other pets.

Dogs

I have seen a wide variety of dogs out hiking and camping, but one thing remains the same among all breeds—they can be reckless if allowed. Even the best-trained dog can get out of control in a stimulating environment or if their owner is not paying attention. Leave No Trace conducted a pet waste study in the city of Boulder, Colorado. Within their observations, they noticed those dog owners who kept their dogs on leash were significantly more likely to bag their pet's waste immediately and were more likely to dispose of the waste bag after picking it up. While this study focuses on pet waste, this stuck out to me because it identified the pet owner's responsibility in regard to other necessary actions, almost like a domino effect (Blenderman et al., 2018).

I was on a hike just a week ago in an area that requires all dogs to be leashed. It was a narrow trail section, heavily overgrown, creating a tunnel effect, and out of nowhere, a large-breed dog came bounding through, throwing my dog and me off the trail. This was partially because we were startled and reacted to an animal running toward us, but also because this dog was not under the control of their owner and very obviously off-leash. It took me a moment to gather myself, and although my dog is easily distracted, with more time on the trail together, he's getting better at reading situations and knows how he should react, so he patiently waited for me, ignoring the other dog. We continued hiking, and it took maybe 5 minutes for us to come upon the owner. What was even more humorous in this situation was that she wasn't paying attention to where she was going, and I startled her when I said hello. She had no awareness of her surroundings, let alone what her dog was up to. This situation creates a dilemma for several reasons: It is dangerous for the dog, wildlife, and other hikers, but it almost guarantees that the dog's poop won't be picked up.

I'm going to be honest, I was her when I first got my dog. I was a terrible dog owner, and the first few times we went hiking, I let him run off-leash, and I often lost him and spent hours trying to find him. I quickly figured out that was not safe for him, it was annoying for me, other hikers hated me, and he was damaging that environment. We have worked on things together, and now we are a happy, responsible hiking pair, but Ash still needs reminders and reinforcement every time we hike. At first, though, I didn't know any better. I didn't realize that it would be harmful to let him have a good time running around on the trails with me because I didn't know there were rules and regulations that applied to pets when hiking.

The good news is that many trail etiquette and Leave No Trace principles apply to humans and dogs. So, as you get to know those yourself, you can implement them with your pet. Beyond the standard Leave No Trace principles that encourage you to pick up dog poop and dispose of it properly, there's more trail etiquette to consider with your dog.

When you are hiking alone, there are circumstances when you stop because someone else has the right of way. Some of these include hikers going uphill, bikers, and horses. When you are hiking with your dog and approaching another hiker or a group of hikers, you are always the one to yield. If there is someone else with a dog, one of you still needs to yield to let the other pass. The reason you yield when you have a dog is that they're dogs, and they're somewhat unpredictable. To perform a yield when hiking with your dog, have your dog heel and use your body as a barrier between your dog and the person passing. You can have your dog sit, but most of the time, it is easy enough to have the dog heel, wait, and let the people pass. This is a bit easier if your dog is on a leash because you are physically in control. If your dog is off-leash, most trails use a distance or "sight" rule, meaning that your dog must be in sight at all times. Know your dog's limitations. If they do not have good recall, don't hike with them off-leash. Your dog needs to be responsive to you, and if they are off-leash, they need to be well trained enough to heel when yielding and stay despite the stimuli of another person or even another dog passing. Obviously you or your dog cannot be perfect, and these things take practice. Ash and I still practice these things when we hike, and we aren't always perfect at it, but consistency is key. As the dog owner, you are additionally responsible for knowing and following area guidelines regarding leash laws.

This trail etiquette becomes important not only for your dog's safety and the safety of others but also for the safety of the ecosystem. When you have your dog on a leash or remain in control when they are off-leash, you are likely keeping them on the trail. Dogs have a prey drive and many dogs love digging. These are endearing but destructive qualities that can damage natural areas. For the same reasons you need to stay on trail, so does your dog, and that starts with your level of attention as an owner and their level of training.

When you decide that you and your dog are ready for a hiking or camping adventure, you will likely look into more gear options. The gear that I have found necessary when I bring my companion along for hiking, backpacking, or camping includes:

Hiking
- Harness
- Leash (runner's leash recommended)
- Poop bags/paper
- Water bottle + bowl
- Treats

Backpacking
- All hiking and camping gear
- Dog food + dog food bag
- Collapsible bowls
- Boots or paw wax
- Saddle bags
- First-aid kit

Camping
- All hiking and backpacking gear
- Sleeping pad or blanket
- Tether
- LED collar light
- Bug spray

*Optional Gear:** dog carrier for small dog breeds, muzzle for aggressive/reactive dogs or dogs in training, dog poop box/belt for carrying waste on long hikes

Some dog breeds will be capable of carrying some of their gear, but likely not all of it. When looking for gear for your dog, perform your gear research in the same manner you would for outdoor gear you use for yourself, and apply the sustainability and environmental evaluations necessary to narrow down eco-friendly company options. Most gear should last the life span of your dog, with the exception of consumables. There are some external circumstances that can damage the item, so repairability or recyclability are important too.

When you are backpacking or camping with your pet, the most realistic option for dog food will be dry food. If you are RVing or car camping with a pet, then wet food is more feasible because you don't have to carry it with you, but it is often harder to clean up and manage. When you take your dog backpacking with you, be sure that you pack enough food to compensate for the additional calories they're burning and that it is food that they are used to. That means that if your dog usually eats wet food, but you want to bring them backpacking and feed them dry food, you need to transition them before your trip and bring extra water, or they are likely to get sick or not eat at all.

If you want to start to transition your dog to a more plant-based diet because of environmental concerns, be sure that you evaluate their diet with a pet nutrition specialist and choose optimized dog foods like Wild Earth and include supplements. While packing dog food in a plastic bag may be the easiest option, it isn't the most environmentally friendly or durable. Choose to invest in a dog food carrying bag, especially if you travel with your pet often.

Besides gear and food, dog poop can be an issue when backpacking and camping, as we've discussed. When you are in the backcountry with your dog, you'll need to pack out their poop. Some areas may allow you to bury their waste in a cathole, but without a waste bag. To do this in the most low-waste (and stink-free) way, get some Pooch Paper and a wet bag used to transport used cloth baby diapers. Pooch Paper does not seal entirely or tie like a poop bag, so if this concerns you, then find out if the area you're traveling has an industrial compost system that accepts compostable dog poop bags. Then, you can pick up your dog's waste and carry it in the wet bag. I recommend packing this wet bag at the bottom of your pack, where you would carry a wag bag for yourself. Although, in theory, these bags shouldn't leak, better safe than sorry, so you want to keep it as far away from your food as possible. If you are hiking in a more developed area, you may not need to prepare quite as much for this because you will come across more trailheads and trash receptacles during your hike.

Cats

While it is far less common than seeing dogs on the hiking trail, I have seen several leash-trained cats out hiking. A couple of my close friends also have a cat that they've taken backpacking and often take car camping. If you are a cat owner whose cat loves to go on outdoor adventures with you, this section is for you.

Like with dogs, plan to pick up your cat's poop when you are out hiking, camping, or backpacking. Their poop is foreign to that ecosystem and should be collected accordingly. You can easily use the same methods you use for picking up dog poop for collecting cat poop. If you are car camping or RV camping, bringing a litter box will help ensure your cat feels comfortable and prevent them from using outdoor areas to go to the bathroom. However, many cat owners who choose to bring their cat backpacking found that towing along a litter box was unnecessary, and they opted to pick up their cat's waste as they went.

Keep your cat on a leash when hiking and camping. This is not only for their safety but also for the safety of wildlife in the area. Your cat likely will enjoy catching and killing wildlife such as birds or mice.

Depending on the length of your hike, you may have to carry your cat for a portion of it. There are cat carrier backpacks that make this easy or even attachments for a backpacking pack to carry them when they get tired. Some cats also do quite well simply perching on the top of your backpack, so it is somewhat up to your cat's temperament and preference here.

As with dogs, adventure cats are only as well behaved as their level of training and enforcement. Although cats might be more challenging to train, they can be trained and enjoy outdoor adventures safely and in a low-waste manner. Still, your cat doesn't need to go everywhere with you, and in some cases they may be better off at home. So just as with dogs, know your cat's limitations and leave them home if that will be a safer environment for them.

When it comes to food and gear with cats, implement the same tactics you would for standard outdoor gear in terms of shopping according to durability and sustainability. Cats don't tend to be quite as rambunctious as dogs when they are outdoors, so gear like harnesses is likely to last longer.

Horses and pack animals

The use of horses and other hoofed creatures like mules, donkeys, and llamas as pack animals can be polarizing in terms of waste problems on hiking trails. When looking at equestrians specifically on shared trails with hikers and bikers, horse manure becomes the key talking point. From a nonequestrian standpoint, equestrians are seen as disrespectful and not abiding by trail etiquette or environmental standards because they leave their horse's poop on the trails. The same can be said for outfitters that use pack animals and let them poop on the trails. Often, the recreationalists that have the most complaints about horse manure on trails are the cyclists. This is because they're the most likely to be slung in the face or get some slicked on their back as they fly down trails.

The most common argument against equestrians leaving horse manure on unpaved hiking trails is, "if people have to pick up dog poop, you should have to pick up horse poop." In theory, this makes some sense. No one likes looking at a pile of horse poop, but how much of an environmental or health hazard is it? We must consider that the primary reason dog poop is such an environmental hazard is because they are omnivores and often eat meat-heavy diets, which create more room for bacteria-ridden poop. On the other hand, horses are herbivores and are considered grazing animals, meaning their diets consist primarily of grasses. When a horse is healthy, their poop shouldn't smell and should dry relatively quickly, allowing it to break down within 2 weeks and disperse in most environments. It also poses far less risk to human health than dog poop (Quinn, 2001).

Yes, it is true that they are still not a part of that ecosystem, so should their waste be left on the trails? While horse poop does break down quickly and does not pose much of a risk to human health, unmanaged manure does pose an environmental risk, especially in high-traffic areas for horses. That's because manure, often used as fertilizer, contains phosphorus and nitrogen. These nutrients can leach into soils and be beneficial, but they can also run off into waterways, polluting ecosystems. When nutrients like nitrogen are not taken up and used by plants, then they are likely to move through the soil to be leached into groundwater. Phosphorus will only leach in the same way if the soil matrix is oversaturated, contaminating surface water. Essentially, the major concern with too much unmanaged manure in isolated areas like hiking trails is that it can run off into surface waters leading to eutrophication (excessive nutrient richness) and oxygen depletion (Westendorf, 2004). This gets tricky, because phosphorus and nitrogen levels will depend on the horse's diet. Horses with high-protein diets often have higher levels of nitrogen but concentrated in their urine.

It isn't always practical or safe for equestrians to dismount and clean up horse poop on the trail. In my opinion, at the very least, guiding companies or trail riding companies should be required to clean up after their tours because they are contributing far more than a single equestrian riding a trail. Some hiking and backcountry areas have specific rules and regulations regarding horse manure and will have manure collection bins or a dispersal requirement.

Most hiking areas that allow horse packing or trail riding require riders to clean up horse poop in staging areas, parking lots, and paved trails. Beyond that, though, they are free to leave the horse poop on the trails. If there is a trail rest stop of some kind, most hiking areas will ask that equestrians scatter the poop off the trail. Some riders will clean up poop if it happens in the beginning section of the trail, and it is easy to go back to from their trailer. However, there isn't necessarily a rule requiring them to do so.

Beyond the manure aspect of horses, their impact on the trail is often in question. While it is true that horses and other hoofed animals create about three times as much wear on a trail as a hiker does, they are still not as impactful as bikes or motorized recreational vehicles like dirt bikes or ATVs.

Other Pets

I've seen people bring rats and bunnies on outdoor adventures. I've seen rabbits harnessed up and hopping happily along the trail, and those that bring their rat companion usually carry them on their pack or shoulder. Small pets like this cause little to no damage unless they are released into the wild, where they are likely to be eaten by predators.

No matter the pet that you bring with you hiking or camping, mindful pet ownership and responsibility for their impact should be the primary focus. It is easy to get distracted doing other activities, especially if you are camping and backpacking, so having systems in place to ensure your pet stays close to you and on the trail will help you continue to keep tabs on them. For small pets like rats, bunnies, and even cats, consider bringing a carrier so you can have a safe place to put them when you can't pay close attention. If you're unsure you'll be able to keep track of them, then it is safest to leave them at home.

Bushcraft and Outdoor Minimalism

BUSHCRAFT IS MOST OFTEN ASSOCIATED WITH WILDERNESS SUR-
vival and is defined in the Oxford dictionary as "skills in matters
pertaining to life in the bush." The term *bushcraft* has been used
historically and in writing since the 1800s, primarily in Australia
and South Africa. It is thought to be an adaptation of several
Dutch phrases used when talking about the Indigenous San
peoples of the Khoe, Tuu, or Kx'a cultures in South Africa and
beyond (Sailer, 2002). Today, bushcraft has evolved to become a
collection of many Indigenous hunter-gatherer cultures and practices pertaining to surviving off the landscape.

At its core, bushcraft uses outdoor skills and knowledge that
allow an individual to survive in natural environments. The most
basic bushcraft skills would then include practical skills like fire
starting, building shelters, foraging, and fishing. There are several
other extensions of bushcraft skills that include natural crafts,
woodworking, and navigation. The best way to think of bushcraft
is any skill or practice that enhances wilderness survival and gives
you self-reliance in a wilderness setting.

Like any outdoor activity, people involved in bushcraft often
have different levels of interest and expertise. For instance, some
survivalists may only venture into the wilderness for wild camping experiences to test and hone their skills by bringing little
to no gear with them. Others dabble in bushcraft skills when
they are camping by practicing natural fire starting methods

or learning how to build traps from natural materials. The level of expertise you seek or have in bushcraft is a spectrum. Still, no matter the amount of knowledge you have in the world of bushcraft, know that those skills overlap dramatically with the concepts of outdoor minimalism.

Both outdoor minimalism and bushcraft take on similar concepts in terms of a "less is more" approach. However, when thinking of the true roots of bushcraft, it is more about making do with what you have versus going without something. It is also about respecting what is provided through nature and never taking more than you need. This is a fundamental mindset shift when considering any minimalist approach to life, and can be applied to any outdoor activity from car camping, to ultralight backpacking, to bushcraft. No matter the pursuit, you can ask yourself the primary question that drives the bulk of this book: *Is this necessary?* When you get to the bare bones of outdoor survival and bushcraft skills, it is about necessity and adaptability in an outdoor environment.

To me, bushcraft can be seen as an extension of outdoor minimalism. As you home in on your outdoor hobbies and identify personal needs, pursuing bushcraft skills becomes about more than simply survival, but it can bring forth a greater appreciation for natural systems, the human experience in relation to nature, and can teach you how little you need to not only survive, but thrive in the wilderness. With that in mind, it is essential to acknowledge that bushcraft is not meant to be a detriment to a landscape, and we should not be encroaching on natural spaces by taking advantage of these resources.

Wilderness survival is not something to be taken lightly, and preparedness and knowledge are essential. While learning about bushcraft, I recommend taking a class or having a mentor of some kind who can guide you through specific skills and implementations of most bushcraft activities to ensure a higher level of competency and safety. These types of instructional courses should also teach you how to minimize your impact when practicing these skills. Then, as you progress in your expertise, you can begin to branch out more independently and likely bring fewer items to assist you.

Both outdoor minimalism and bushcraft require an intense focus on slowing down and observing your surroundings as well as your personal behaviors. With bushcraft, the need to be observant and adaptable comes more into play, but there is still a high level of self-awareness and the expectation that nature will humble you. The reason that I decided to include an introduction to bushcraft in this book is that it is a natural progression in the outdoor minimalist journey. Yes, it is true that many readers will not gravitate toward bushcraft activities of any kind, but having a base level knowledge of some basic survival skills can be a very empowering and practical experience.

INTRO TO BUSHCRAFT SKILLS EVERYONE SHOULD KNOW

In theory, bushcraft would allow you to survive in the wilderness with little to nothing but your body. Most bushcraft experts often include a knife as a necessity, but you can also learn skills like flint knapping to make weapons and tools of your own. Everyone will have their threshold when it comes to their comfort level regarding survival or bushcraft.

Some of the most basic bushcraft skills that any outdoor adventurer can benefit from knowing include:

- Fire making
- Building a shelter
- Collecting and purifying water
- Hunting and foraging
- Land navigation
- Treating wounds and first aid

- Tracking
- Knot tying and rope making

Most of these skills you will not learn overnight, and it will take persistence to become proficient in them. Many of the most experienced people in the world of bushcraft have been practicing wilderness survival for years. Still, certain skills like knot tying, fire making, and even navigation can be learned in a matter of days or hours with the proper instruction and dedication. Just knowing the concepts often is not enough to get you by with bushcraft, though, and these skills must be put into action to reach true proficiency and confidence in your ability.

Bushcraft helps you shift your dependence away from store-bought and man-made items when exploring the outdoors. If you are interested in pursuing bushcraft skills as a way to add to your wilderness knowledge, I recommend finding an outdoor school near you and investing in bushcraft books such as Dave Canterbury's *Bushcraft 101: A Field Guide to the Art of Wilderness Survival* or Mors Kochanski's *Bushcraft: Outdoor Skills and Wilderness Survival*. These are both wonderful introductions to the world of bushcraft and a great place to start to gauge your level of interest. Then, I recommend Dave Canterbury's follow-up book, *Advanced Bushcraft*, which introduces more advanced bushcraft and survival skills.

Leave It Better Than You Found It

LEAVING AN AREA BETTER THAN YOU FOUND IT IS COVERED briefly within the "Seven Rs of Outdoor Minimalism" chapter, but it deserves more attention than I could give it there. Most of the information up until this point is mainly preventative or specific ways to lessen environmental impact. While those are essential practices within a minimalist lifestyle, keep in mind that anytime you venture out into the wilderness, you disrupt wildlife and alter that ecosystem no matter the activity. How much you impact that ecosystem is dependent on your awareness and ability to follow the Leave No Trace principles and ethics (covered at the beginning of the book). We need to be proactive to offset the unavoidable impact of our presence in the outdoors. Usually this takes the form of picking up garbage, trash, and other evidence of recent human activity.

The concept of leaving an area better than you found it consists of two major pieces:

1. Packing out trash you bring in.

2. Picking up trash you find along the way.

PACK IT IN, PACK IT OUT

One of my biggest pet peeves anytime I am hiking, paddling, biking, camping, or basically doing anything outside is seeing trash blow around or float on by. No, actually, that's not my biggest pet peeve. The biggest one is watching someone litter on the trail. During my first ultramarathon race, I remember running behind a man for a few miles, and during that time, he decided to eat one of his energy snacks. It was an energy goo of some kind that came in a single-serve container. To my surprise, after he consumed it, he casually tossed the trash onto the trail. I stopped because I was kind of surprised that someone would do that during a race, and I picked it up and put it in my running belt.

As many outdoor enthusiasts know, that is not an uncommon occurrence. If it were uncommon, then we wouldn't need organizations like Clean Trails organizing trail cleanups on a regular basis. Yes, sometimes, when trash ends up on a trail, it is an accident. I'm sure that I've accidentally lost trash from it blowing out of my car door or falling out of my pack without me noticing. Things happen, and we can't be perfect, but we can be more mindful. As you begin to minimize the number of single-use wrappers and packages that you bring into the outdoors, you will become less likely to litter in the first place because you won't have as much garbage. There will still always be a handful of items that you need to pack out.

To avoid losing track of any garbage you may accumulate, have a designated collection bag for your camping and backpacking trash. This can be a plastic bag, but ideally, it would be a reusable bag of some kind. For instance, Stasher recommends reusing their silicone food bags as trash collection bags once they are no longer suitable for food (i.e., they get a small hole or puncture). You may need something that seals completely, though, so if you carry out something like coffee grounds, they aren't leaking in your pack. I have mentioned the use of wet bags in other chapters, but honestly, they are one of the best options for carrying out waste in the backcountry. They are designed to transport dirty cloth diapers, so they are waterproof, conceal the smell, and are machine washable. They come in a variety of sizes, allowing you to invest in them according to your needs: for instance, if you need a small travel-size bag for food waste versus a larger bag to carry out your dog's waste. If you have an infant that you bring into the backcountry, then these are a necessity for their diapers. There are also specialty dry sacks designed for carrying out trash that tend to be more durable for outdoor use that I'd recommend for longer excursions like thru-hikes.

There have been times when I've forgotten to pack a trash collection bag, which is why preparedness is a necessity in this situation. Luckily, since I often backpack or hike with my dog, I can use one of his poop bags in those instances to hold and collect my trash. In these types of situations, it is best not to blame yourself for the mistake and to make do with the resources you have available to you at the time. Using a poop bag isn't a perfect solution, but it is better than leaving trash on the trail or at a campsite. A large part of outdoor experiences is improvising and innovation, but it is also about responsibility. By taking responsibility for not only yourself but your impact on the environment you pass through, you engage in an empowering relationship with the natural world.

Pick It Up

Beyond taking responsibility for your trash when outdoors, sometimes there comes a point when you also need to take responsibility for other people's trash. This is an unfortunate reality of our world, but people often wonder how effective litter collection is. There are some area cleanups on beaches or trails that occur monthly or even weekly, and still, they have to return again and again to find more and more trash. That cycle can make even the most dedicated cleanup crews lose a bit of momentum and hope.

Much like the piling of dog poop bags under a signpost or even tossing a banana peel to the side of the trail, trash begets more trash. What I mean by this is that if you are hiking along carrying your dog poop bag and you see a pile of bags or even one or two by the side of the trail, it makes you feel justified putting down the poop bag with the others. The same goes for littering a wrapper of any kind. If you see an area with a lot of trash scattered about, it becomes easier for you to justify to yourself that you can litter in that area. On the other hand, if an area is clean and no trash is to be seen, there is a bit more sub-conscious pressure to put that wrapper in your pocket or bring it to a trash bin instead of littering.

If you get used to visiting a trail that always has trash on it, it will inspire you to either clean up or just let it be because that's just the way it always is. Much like littering inspires more litter-ing, cleaning up can inspire more cleaning up. Many people feel somewhat helpless within the environmental movement. It feels like the issues are too big and too far beyond our control for us to have an impact. Realistically, picking up one energy bar wrapper on a day hike isn't going to reverse climate change, but it can prevent a bird or turtle from eating it or making its way into the nearest water source. In this sense, you are adopting Jane Good-all's approach to "think globally, but act locally."

If every person who passes by a piece of litter has the mental-ity that it is someone else's problem, the trash will never be picked up. If you want to do this on a hike but don't want to carry around a plastic bag each time, then invest in a reusable bag of some kind that you can use to collect and then deposit trash into a waste bin at the trailhead or parking area. There are several options for a reusable bag to collect trash, including the Clean Earth Bag released by Fish Gods LLC in 2020. Their bag is tear-resistant, mold/mildew resistant, and has an adjustable size. You can easily attach it to your pack, and it is easy to keep clean. If you are mak-ing cleaning up trails a habit as you hike, then it is a great idea to have a designated bag you can use instead of bringing a new plastic bag each time you go.

Sometimes, litter occurs unintentionally, and a large percentage of litter is seen within 5 meters of a trash bin. This can happen for several reasons, such as someone missing the trash bin when tossing something, or perhaps there isn't a lid, and it blows out of the trash receptacle. Most litter that starts on land makes its way to the water, whether it blows into a river to be carried to a larger body of water or is swept in storm drains. Within the United States and Canada, it is estimated that around 10,000 metric tons of plastic waste enter water systems like lakes or rivers each year (UNFCCC, 2020). That number only counts plastic litter in two countries in the entire world, so we can safely assume there is far more trash that starts out as litter on land that is swept into water.

Essentially all plastic created since the 1950s is still in the environment one way or another, and more plastic products are produced each day (Geyer, Jambeck, and Law, 2017). Whenever something is littered, it either biodegrades or breaks down into smaller pieces over time, leading to pollution not visible to the naked eye. The majority of litter is food and drink packages or cigarette butts, and these types of materials don't degrade quickly, and some won't degrade within our lifetime.

How long it takes for litter to break down or decompose depends on several factors, including the type and quality of the material itself, the climate of the region where it is littered, and geographical location. Things like more moisture or sun exposure often cause materials to degrade much faster, which is why decomposition rates of materials vary so dramatically in different locations or when comparing litter decomposition to the breakdown of trash in a landfill setting. Then, even within the landfill setting, there are variables that contribute to the rate of material breakdown.

Litter Type	Rate of Decomposition in the Environment
Paper Towel	2–4 weeks
Newspaper	6 weeks
Tetra Pak or Wax Carton	3 months
Plywood	1–3 years
Wool Fabric	1–5 years
Cigarette Butt	5+ years
Plastic* Bag	20+ years
Firm Plastic Container	30+ years
Nylon Fabric	40+ years
Leather	50 years
Tin Can	50 years
Rubber	50–80 years
Foamed Plastic Cup	50+ years
Aluminum Can	80–200 years
Disposable Diapers	450+ years
Plastic Bottle	450+ years
Monofilament Fishing Line	600+ years
Glass Bottle	1 million years

Not all materials, like plastic, will ever truly decompose or biodegrade without the proper environment. They continue to break down into smaller pieces to eventually become microplastics, making them harder to remove.

Information Source: US National Park Service

By and large, trash degrades much faster as litter than in most landfill settings, and that is because of the compact nature of landfills. There is minimal exposure to dirt, water, oxygen, and sunlight in a landfill, creating an anaerobic environment that preserves trash for longer periods of time. When petroleum is turned into plastic, it is no longer biodegradable without chemical intervention and can stay preserved in a landfill setting nearly indefinitely.

On top of the rate of trash decomposition, landfills present various other environmental concerns in terms of greenhouse gases and toxins leaching into the ground soil. That's why when

Reasons Not to Leave Litter When You See It

1. It is an eyesore! Keep trails and communities inviting and beautiful by cleaning up litter.

2. Litter damages the environment and ecosystem in various ways, including polluting waterways, harming wildlife, and inhibiting plant growth.

3. Improperly disposed trash can become a carrier and distributor of diseases, viruses, and parasites through direct and indirect contact.

4. Litter begets litter.

we are collecting trash of any kind, it is important to distribute it to the appropriate waste management system to prevent a continuous buildup of trash and to encourage the appropriate redistribution or decomposition of materials.

JOIN A LOCAL CLEANUP

Education and awareness are two of the most effective ways to influence individual action in terms of litter. Cleanups have shown to be wonderful ways to engage community members and keep natural areas clean. Cleanups are an extremely important part of the environmental movement because of the damages that litter causes to natural systems, but should only be seen as a Band-Aid on a much larger issue.

Solutions to our waste problem are often reactive and focused on management, not prevention. Cleanups on land do prevent waste from getting to the ocean, and while this is a positive response, going about "business as usual" may not be the most effective approach. When talking about solving specifically the plastic waste problem, we may need to focus more on changing

Systems Solutions to Plastic Pollution

- invest in circular recycling and waste management systems,
- extend environmental responsibility to producers,
- stop fossil fuel subsidies,
- limit and regulate virgin plastic production,
- align and regulate global production standards, and
- organize and implement trash cleanup efforts in all ecosystems.

(Lau et al.)

production systems as opposed to waste collecting, recycling, and disposal systems. A system change should be one that is not only addressing the plastic waste as a consumer issue but in a way that reduces the amount of virgin plastic put into production and increases recycled plastic feedstock. Essentially, less plastic is produced, therefore, less plastic is littered. As the production goes down, the demand for plastic also lowers and the amount of plastic items and microplastics entering ecosystems naturally declines. The system change scenario, in theory, moves our production systems toward a more circular economy in an effort to minimize waste generation in conjunction with a reduction of consumption (Lau et al., 2020).

We should look at cleanups as a way to raise awareness that turns into tangible action. Area cleanups often inspire people to get more involved in environmental efforts and can create a domino effect in terms of eco-conscious living and habits. As an individual, cleaning up a trail alone can feel demoralizing, but we often impact the people around us, helping bring them more awareness of these important environmental issues.

There are a variety of organizations globally, nationally, and locally that host cleanups. Specific organizations like Clean Trails and National CleanUp Day focus on organizing cleanups in outdoor recreation areas, but other organizations like Rubbish tend to focus on city cleanups. You don't need to be associated with an organization to make a change though! You can pick up trash on daily walks and hikes, organize with friends and family, and check with local parks and recreation departments to see where they need volunteers for cleanups or if they host events. No matter the organization you get involved with, cleanups are a great way to inspire action in your community.

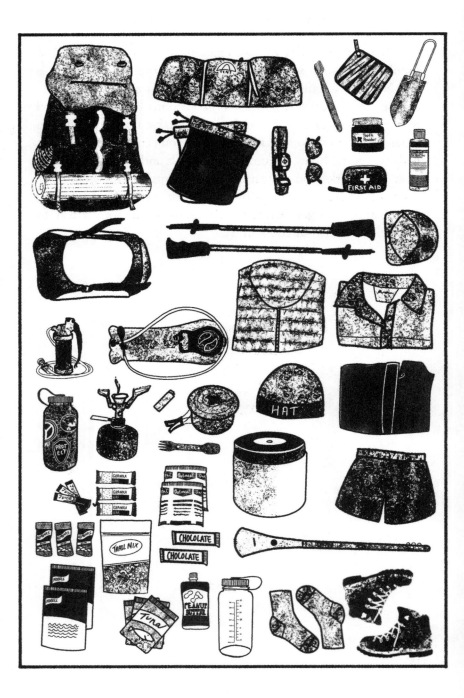

Packing Lists

ANY TYPE OF OUTDOOR TRAVEL BECOMES FAR MORE ENJOYABLE, safer, and sustainable when you are fully prepared. A part of being prepared includes planning transportation, knowing the area you're traveling, studying maps if going into the backcountry, and understanding how to navigate the landscape. The other part of planning comes down to packing the right things. In terms of outdoor minimalism, having a specific plan for the gear you need to bring not only helps you feel safe and secure in an outdoor setting, but it also gives you a starting point for gear and equipment shopping.

No matter the type of outdoor endeavor, pack for the climate and weather conditions. Invest time before your trip to learn about that specific environment and any potential environmental hazards that may be in that area (e.g., bears, venomous snakes, poisonous plants, dangerous weather patterns). If you are spending time in a state or national park, consult the rangers of that park about the current trail and weather conditions. If there aren't rangers to consult, contact local outfitters and get their recommendations and advice. This not only gives you the knowledge of what to expect, but it also gives you an opportunity to address any last-minute gear concerns or make changes.

Note: All packing lists will have some overlap and variation according to personal preferences and needs. Use this section of the book as a launching pad for your trip planning and alter the lists according to your needs and the length of your trip.

Day Hiking
- ☐ Backpack or fanny pack for short hikes
- ☐ Hiking shoes
- ☐ Water and snacks
- ☐ Knife/multitool
- ☐ First-aid kit
- ☐ Sunscreen and bug spray
- ☐ Appropriate clothing for climate/weather
- ☐ Optional for location: navigation tools

Car Camping and RV Camping
- ☐ Tent or shelter
- ☐ Sleeping pad, cot, or camping air mattress
  - ☐ Inflation tool (if needed)
- ☐ Sleeping bag or blankets
- ☐ Camping pillow
- ☐ Headlamp and lantern
- ☐ Camp chairs
- ☐ Firewood and fire starter
- ☐ Toiletries
- ☐ Climate- and weather-appropriate clothing
- ☐ Camp kitchen items
  - ☐ Stove
  - ☐ Fuel
  - ☐ Pots/pans

- ☐ Cutting board
- ☐ Spatula
- ☐ Knife
- ☐ Utensils
- ☐ Plates/bowls
- ☐ Cups/mugs
- ☐ Dish towel
- ☐ Biodegradable soap
- ☐ Cooler
- ☐ Water container
- ☐ Trash bags
- ☐ Camp sink
- ☐ Oil and spices (if cooking over fire: roasting sticks, tin foil, dutch oven)
- ☐ Camp comfort items
  - ☐ Hammock
  - ☐ Camp chairs
  - ☐ Camp table
  - ☐ Lights/bug candles
  - ☐ Clothesline
  - ☐ Shade tent/tarp
- ☐ Camp tools
  - ☐ Multitool/knife
  - ☐ Mallet
  - ☐ Hatchet
  - ☐ Saw
  - ☐ Broom and dustpan

- [ ] Optional
  - [ ] Camp games
  - [ ] Journal
  - [ ] Binoculars
  - [ ] Camera
  - [ ] Musical instruments
  - [ ] Portable charger
  - [ ] Solar panels and power bank
  - [ ] Grill

Weekend Backpacking Trip

- [ ] Backpack
- [ ] Pack rain cover
- [ ] Sleeping shelter
- [ ] Sleeping pad
- [ ] Sleeping bag
- [ ] Headlamp
- [ ] Backpacking stove and fuel
- [ ] Lighter
- [ ] Mess kit
- [ ] Stuff sacks/dry bags
- [ ] Water purification/filter
- [ ] Water bladder and bottles
- [ ] Biodegradable soap
- [ ] Towel
- [ ] Food and water
- [ ] Toiletries
- [ ] Emergency kit

- ☐ First-aid kit
- ☐ Climate- and weather-appropriate clothing
- ☐ Location dependent: bear canister or bear bag, bear spray

Ultralight Backpacking

- ☐ Sleeping bag (down is lightest, 750 fill or better)
- ☐ 60-inch closed foam sleeping pad
- ☐ Internal frame backpack or frameless (2 pounds or less)
- ☐ Siliconized nylon tarp and trekking poles for tent support
- ☐ Water bladder and bottle
- ☐ Water treatment (chlorine dioxide or iodine)
- ☐ Canister or alcohol stove with lighter and fuel
- ☐ Titanium or ultralight aluminum cooking pot
- ☐ Spork and knife
- ☐ Toiletries
- ☐ Navigation tools
- ☐ Small LED headlamp
- ☐ Sunscreen and bug spray
- ☐ Siliconized nylon stuff sacks
- ☐ First-aid kit
- ☐ Location dependent: bear canister or bear bag, bear spray

Long-Distance Backpacking (Thru Hiking)

- ☐ Backpack and rain cover
- ☐ Shelter of choice
- ☐ Sleeping bag
- ☐ Sleeping pad
- ☐ Trekking poles

- [ ] Stuff sacks/dry bags
- [ ] Headlamp
- [ ] Camp stove and fuel
- [ ] Lighter
- [ ] Mess kit
- [ ] Toiletries
- [ ] Water treatment
- [ ] Water reservoir and water bottle
- [ ] First-aid kit
- [ ] Gear repair kit
- [ ] Navigation tools
- [ ] Climate- and weather-appropriate clothing
- [ ] Hiking shoes (recommended: trail runners and gaiters)
- [ ] Location dependent: bear canister or bear bag, bear spray, microspikes
- [ ] Optional: camping pillow, bug net

Bike Touring and Bikepacking
- [ ] Bike Gear
  - [ ] Bike
  - [ ] Helmet
  - [ ] Bike packs/panniers
  - [ ] Headlight
  - [ ] Taillight
  - [ ] Bike lock
  - [ ] Optional: navigation mount
- [ ] Shelter of choice (tent, hammock, tarp, bivouac sack)
- [ ] Sleeping bag

- ☐ Sleeping pad
- ☐ Camp kitchen
  - ☐ Stove
  - ☐ Fuel
  - ☐ Lighter/matches
  - ☐ Cooking pot
  - ☐ Mug
  - ☐ Spork
  - ☐ Knife
- ☐ Water treatment with reservoir and bottles
- ☐ Appropriate clothing for both biking and when in camp
- ☐ Toiletries
- ☐ Navigation tools
  - ☐ Map
  - ☐ Compass
  - ☐ Phone
  - ☐ Bike computer/GPS
  - ☐ Personal location beacon
  - ☐ Portable charger
  - ☐ Necessary permits
- ☐ Bike repair tools
  - ☐ Tubes
  - ☐ Compact pump/CO_2 inflator with cartridges
  - ☐ Tire patch kit
  - ☐ Bike multitool
  - ☐ Chain tool (if not on multitool)
  - ☐ Replacement chain links

☐ Tire levers

☐ Spare spokes

☐ Spoke wrench

☐ Chain lubricant

☐ Zip ties

☐ Duct tape

☐ 6-inch adjustable wrench

☐ Brake and derailleur cables

☐ For tubeless tires: extra tire tape and sealant

☐ First-aid kit

☐ Headlamp

Canoe, Kayak, or Stand Up Paddleboard (SUP) Camping
Be prepared for some variation depending on the type of watercraft you choose.

☐ Water vessel of choice

☐ PFD (personal flotation device)

☐ Paddle and spare paddle

☐ Bowline

☐ Paddle float and other rescue gear

☐ Bilge pump and bailer

☐ Deck light

☐ Kayak cockpit cover

☐ First-aid kit

☐ Repair kit

☐ Spare clips, cleats, bungee cords, and parachute cord

☐ Tent/shelter

- [ ] Sleep system
- [ ] Water treatment with reservoir and bottle
- [ ] Toiletries
- [ ] Headlamp and batteries
- [ ] Camp kitchen and mess kit
- [ ] Knife
- [ ] Navigation tools
- [ ] Dry sack and waterproof bags
- [ ] Optional: fishing gear, foam pads for kneeling in canoe

Sea Travel–Specific Items
- [ ] Bowlines
- [ ] Sponge and bailer
- [ ] Paddle float
- [ ] Radio
- [ ] Signal flare
- [ ] Nautical charts and maps

River/Lake Travel–Specific Items
- [ ] Pin kit
- [ ] Groover
- [ ] Portage duffel
- [ ] Guide book or navigation tools
- [ ] Whitewater: helmet

Beginner Bushcraft Kit
- [ ] Backpack
- [ ] Axe or hatchet
- [ ] Knife

☐ Water purification or filter

☐ Fire starting gear

☐ Tarp and paracord

☐ Sleeping bag and pad

☐ Navigation tools

☐ Mess kit

☐ Headlamp

☐ Necessary toiletries

☐ Food (beginner bushcrafters are assumed to bring their own backpacking food but can opt to include fishing as part of their meals)

☐ Climate- and weather-appropriate clothing

☐ Location dependent: camp stove

Meg's Sustainable Brand Picks

Buying gear secondhand—whether it be in a consignment shop, from a friend, or online—is one of the most sustainable gear purchasing options. If you cannot find the gear that fits your needs used, then consider one of the following brands when purchasing new gear.

Many of the companies on this list are big-name brands that distribute to a wide audience, but there are some smaller companies on the list. Shop local when you can, but accessibility is an issue with strictly listing local brands. So, do your research and if you can't source it sustainably and locally, branch out from there.

- **Backpacks:** Osprey, Gregory, REI
- **Bikepacks:** Green Guru Gear
- **Hiking Shoes:** Merrell, Mammut, Altra, Xero Shoes
- **Outdoor Clothing:** Ottomatic Threads, Patagonia, Cotopaxi, Picture Organics, Prana, Corbeaux, Burgeon Outdoor, Appalachian Gear Company
- **Water Bladders/Reservoirs:** CNOC Outdoors, MSR Dromedary
- **Water Filters:** Katadyn BeFree (42mm), Hydroblu Versa Flow (28mm)
- **Dry Bags/Stuff Sacks:** Sea to Summit
- **Trekking Poles:** CNOC Outdoors
- **Tent:** Vaude, Big Agnes, The North Face, Kelty
- **Bivvy:** Outdoor Research
- **Sleeping Pad:** Vaude, Therm-a-Rest (foam pads)
- **Sleeping Bag:** NEMO Equipment, REI
- **Mess Kit:** MSR, GSI Outdoors
- **Stove:** MSR liquid fuel
- **Reusable Food Packaging:** Khala & CO

(continued)

Meg's Sustainable Brand Picks (*continued*)

- **Water Bottles:** CNOC Outdoors, Klean Kanteen, Tree Tribe, Hydroflask
- **Pee Rag:** Wander Women Gear
- **Trekking Towel:** Lava Linens
- **Climbing Gear:** Edelrid, Sterling Ropes, La Sportiva, ORGANIC Climbing, Kush Climbing, Petzl, Metolius

Dog-Specific Brand Picks

- **Dog Poop Bags:** Pooch Paper
- **Harness:** Only Natural Pet
- **Leash:** Crag Dog
- **Collar:** The Good Dog Company
- **Boots:** Kurgo
- **Coat:** Kurgo, Ruffwear
- **Sleeping Bag:** Ruffwear

Conclusion

We abuse land because we see it as a commodity belonging to us. When we see land as a community to which we belong, we may begin to use it with love and respect.

—ALDO LEOPOLD

ENVIRONMENTALISM AND SUSTAINABILITY IN ANY FORM IS A journey, not an endpoint. Much like hiking, biking, or paddling, far more is gained from enjoying the present moment than fixating on the summit or destination. That's not to say that having goals and tangible solutions are irrelevant, far from it. I am saying that a growth mindset can be applied even when we discuss concepts like minimalism. Growing and expanding isn't always based on the physical but can also be conceptual and rooted in a mission far beyond ourselves.

Outdoor minimalism extends existing ideas like zero-waste, circular economies, and the Leave No Trace principles and ethics. It is not necessarily groundbreaking or wholly new and unique. Still, it is an essential and distinct approach that brings a more targeted focus to the responsibility the outdoor recreation communities and the outdoor industry have to protect and restore our natural spaces. Environmental protection is often discussed in outdoor circles, but it can easily get lost within the need for commercial growth and fiscal sustainability. Outdoor minimalism, at its core, is meant to challenge conventional consumer concepts and our "buy more" culture. It is about finding wonder in the expanse of our minds as we enjoy the natural world in a safe, comfortable manner, and finding that we need far less than we often believe.

It can feel like one person cannot make a difference, especially when so much environmental damage is caused by a few specific industries and production companies. But that doesn't mean that we have no impact at all and that we cannot influence positive change. I have often felt discouraged when evaluating the state of many ecological communities and lose sight of purpose in those moments. There are several ways to look at and approach these feelings of despair, and it is easy to get lost within eco-anxiety, making you feel alone and insignificant. We need to remember that the environmental movement is just that, a movement. It is a place of momentum and change, driven forward by individuals who bring people together to create a community with a common goal.

Working together is the only way forward if we want to make lasting change, and that starts with each individual's willingness to implement change in all aspects of their lives. Your impact as just one person influences everyone around you, and it continues to trickle down to the people in their lives and beyond. So no, picking up a plastic bottle you see on a daily walk might not feel like it will change the world, but you are setting an example for everyone around you and helping to establish a new normal that pushes back against complacent acceptance of mismanaged systems.

As an outdoor recreationalist, I believe that it is our responsibility, far beyond that of other sectors of society, to support, protect, and restore wild spaces, even if it is in the selfish interest of sustaining a space to enjoy our favorite hobbies. Throughout my life, I have felt the strongest sense of belonging in the wilderness within areas far outside the reach of what we now know as a modern society. Those secret corners without phone service—these are the places where we can rediscover the roots of what it means to be human and become a part of something more. Much like

Aldo Leopold states in the quote above, I see myself as a part of something there. I am a part of an ecological community that I love dearly and have the utmost respect for. I do not own nature, I am a part of it, and to sustain myself as a human being, I must work to sustain all other beings, whether they are sentient or not.

In the end, I hope you can take at least one thing from this book that makes making more sustainable choices easier in your outdoor pursuits. Whether it be how you evaluate gear purchases, the type of food you bring on your next hike, or remembering to pick up your dog's poop, it all has an impact. We have the choice in how much of an impact we make, and what we choose along the way can minimize harm to the planet and all of its inhabitants.

Additional Resources

These are the certifications to look for when buying from sustainable brands and outdoor companies.

Animal Welfare Certifications

Leather Working Group (LWG): Member businesses are audited at every step of the leather supply chain. leatherworkinggroup.com

Leaping Bunny: Certified cruelty-free brands commit to not testing products on animals at any stage of development. leaping bunny.org

Responsible Down Standard (RDS), Responsible Wool Standard (RWS): Administered by Textile Exchange; Certifies responsible sourcing of down and wool, humane treatment of geese, ducks, and sheep in supply chain. textileexchange.org

Vegan Certified: Products contain no animal products, byproducts, or animal-derived materials and have not been tested on animals. vegan.org/certification

Product Certifications

Bluesign: Certifies textiles for environmental impact, workplace safety, consumer protection. bluesign.com/en

Cradle to Cradle Certified (C2C): Covers material health, circularity, clean air and climate protection, water and soil stewardship, and social fairness at the product level. c2ccertified.org

Fair Trade: Labor, environmental, ethical standards that prohibit slavery and child labor, promote sustainability, support farmworkers, and mandate fair wages, safe and fair working conditions. fairtradecertified.org

Fairtrade International: Fairly produced and traded products; traceable supply chains. fairtradeamerica.org

Forest Stewardship Council: Paper and wood products sourced from certified sustainably managed forests that promote and protect biodiversity, benefit lives of local people and workers, and sustain economic viability. fsc.org

Global Organic Textile Standard (GOTS): Organic fibers certified based on ecological and social criteria, independent third-party supply-chain certification. globalstandard.org

OEKO-TEX: Textile safety standard; certifies fabrics are free of harmful chemicals, safe for humans. okeo.tex.com

Protect Land + Sea: Personal care product does not contain environmental pollutants. haereticus-lab.org/protect-land-sea-certification-3/

Recycled Content Certification: Certified measurement of recycled content as a percentage of product. scsglobalservices.com/services/recycled-content-certification

Reef Friendly or Reef Safe: Sunscreen or topical cosmetic free from ingredients, preservatives, and additives found to be toxic to coral reefs. biorius.com/cosmetics-certifications/reef-friendly-certification/

Sustainable Forestry Initiative (SFI): Certifies products made from forests based on measures to protect water quality, biodiversity, wildlife, and environmental conservation. forests.org

BRAND CERTIFICATIONS

Carbon Neutral Certified: Certification process that helps companies measure their carbon footprint, offset carbon emissions, and put plans into place to reduce or eliminate future emissions. carbonneutral.org

Certified B Corporation: Holistic social and environmental impact certification for companies based on verified performance, legal accountability, and transparency. bcorporation.net

Green America's Green Business Certification: Certified commitment to using business as a platform for social change through social justice, environmental sustainability, and transparency. greenamerica.org

1% for the Planet: Companies pledged to donate at least 1 percent of gross sales to environmental nonprofits. onepercentfortheplanet.org

AGRICULTURAL CERTIFICATIONS

Demeter Biodynamic: Certifies organic farming practices with higher standards for holistic, ecological, ethical farming; requirements for fertility, on-farm solutions for disease, pest, and weed control, water conservation, and biodiversity. demeter-usa.org

Marine Stewardship Council: Certifies marine and freshwater organisms sourced from effectively managed fisheries that do not deplete species habitats and minimize environmental impact. msc.org

Non-GMO Project Verified: Wholesale and consumer goods made by brands with verified systems in place to minimize and avoid genetically modified organism contamination via testing, traceability, segregation, formulation, labeling, and quality assurance. nongmoproject.org/product-verification/the-standard

Rainforest Alliance Certified: Farm and forest products sourced, made, and sold sustainably according to farm and supply chain requirements. rainforest-alliance.org

Roundtable on Sustainable Palm Oil (RSPO): Certifies responsible sourcing of palm oil across complex supply chain. rspo.org

USDA National Organic Program: Agricultural production that minimizes synthetic materials and promotes resource recycling and ecological balance. usda.gov/topics/organic

To close the loop, divert waste from going to landfills, and prevent further virgin material extraction, buying secondhand is a necessary part of an outdoor minimalist lifestyle. While I encourage you to look for gear consignment shops within your local community, there are other places to find quality gear and outdoor clothing. Buying used outdoor equipment not only helps the environment, but it can help close the gap and make outdoor recreation more accessible no matter your financial situation.

Where to Buy Used Gear and Equipment

- Patagonia Worn Wear
- REI Good & Used
- Arc'teryx Used Gear
- The North Face Renewed
- Geartrade
- Isella Outdoor
- Switchbackr
- Out&Back
- Rerouted.co
- Outdoor Gear Exchange (gearx)
- Online Goods Exchange Platforms: Facebook Marketplace, craigslist, eBay, etc.

COMPANIES AND ORGANIZATIONS MENTIONED IN THE TEXT*

Clean Trails: international 501(c)3 nonprofit organization with a worldwide community of people dedicated to keeping our wild places and the trails that access those spaces free of litter.

CNOC Outdoors: outdoor gear company manufacturing trekking poles, hydration systems, and more in Portland, Oregon.

CragDog: company repurposing used climbing equipment into gear for dogs based out of Duluth, Minnesota.

Fish Gods LLC: creators of an easy to wear trash collection bag you can use on hikes.

Great Lakes Gear Exchange: used gear consignment store based out of Duluth, Minnesota.

Green Guru: company making gear and bike bags by upcycling materials like bike tubes, tents, and wetsuits based out of Boulder, Colorado.

Khala & CO: low-waste reusable food storage option made from cloth and wax materials. Based in Frederick, Colorado.

Lava Linens: women-owned company that produces a rugged outdoor towel made from flax linen using sustainable practices based out of Boulder, Colorado.

Metamorphic Gear: outdoor and travel gear company that makes products by upcycling them out of sailing equipment.

National CleanUp Day: globally recognized day for individuals and organizations to get out and clean up. It falls on the third Saturday in September every year and was started by the founders of Clean Trails.

Pooch Paper: plastic-free alternative to dog poop bags made in the United States from recycled paper.

Rubbish: mobile app designed to track trash as you pick it up to provide data for areas that may need more infrastructure like trash bins and dog poop stations.

Stasher: reusable silicone food bag

*Listed alphabetically, not in the order of appearance.

REFERENCES

INTRODUCTION
United States Environmental Protection Agency (EPA). "How Communities Have Defined Zero-Waste." 2021. https://www.epa.gov/transforming -waste-tool/how-communities-have-defined-zero-waste.

THE SEVEN RS OF OUTDOOR MINIMALISM
Environmental Defense Fund. "Methane: A Crucial Opportunity in the Climate Fight." 2021. https://www.edf.org/climate/methane-crucial -opportunity-climate-fight.

Vasarhelyi, Kayla. "The Hidden Damage of Landfills." University of Colorado–Boulder Environmental Center. 2021. https://www.colorado.edu/ecenter /2021/04/15/hidden-damage-landfills.

GET TO KNOW YOUR GEAR
Bringezu, S., A. Ramaswami, H. Schandl, M. O'Brien, et al. "Assessing Global Resource Use: A Systems Approach to Resource Efficiency and Pollution Reduction." A Report of the International Resource Panel. United Nations Environment Programme. Nairobi, Kenya. 2017.

Chamas, Ali, Hyunjin Moon, Jiajia Zheng, Yang Qiu, et al. "Degradation Rates of Plastic in the Environment." *ACS Sustainable Chemistry & Engineering* 8, no. 9 (2020), 3494–3511. DOI: 10.1021/acssuschemeng.9b06635.

Ellen MacArthur Foundation. "Vision of a Circular Economy for Fashion." 2020. https://emf.thirdlight.com/link/nbwff6ugh01m-y15u3p/@ /preview/1?o.

Haggith, Mandy, Susan Kinsella, Sergio Baffoni, Patrick Anderson, et al. "The State of the Global Paper Industry: Shifting Seas: New Challenges for Forests, People, and the Climate." Global Paper Network. 2018. https:// environmentalpaper.org/wp-content/uploads/2018/04/StateOfThe GlobalPaperIndustry2018_FullReport-Final-1.pdf.

Sustainable Packaging Coalition: A GreenBlue Project. "Definition of Sustainable Packaging." 2011. https://sustainablepackaging.org/wp-content/uploads/2017/09/Definition-of-Sustainable-Packaging.pdf.

RETHINK TRAIL FOOD
Brooks, Amy L., Shell Wang, and Jenna R. Jambeck. "The Chinese Import Ban and Its Impact on Global Plastic Waste Trade." *Science Advances* 4, no. 6 (June 20, 2018). DOI: 10.1126/sciadv.aat0131.

Gerber, P. J., H. Steinfeld, B. Henderson, A. Mottet, et al. "Tackling Climate Change through Livestock: A Global Assessment of Emissions and Mitigation Opportunities." Food and Agriculture Organization of the United Nations (FAO). 2013.

German, R. N., C. E. Thompson, and T. G. Benton. "Relationships Among Multiple Aspects of Agriculture's Environmental Impact and Productivity: A Meta-Analysis to Guide Sustainable Agriculture." *Biological Reviews* 92, no. 2 (2017), 716–38.

Gustavsson, G., C. Cederberg, U. Sonesson, and A. Emanuelsson. "The Methodology of the FAO Study: 'Global Food Losses and Food Waste—Extent, Causes and Prevention.'" Swedish Institute for Food and Biotechnology (SIK) Report 857. Food and Agriculture Organization of the United Nations(FAO). 2011.

Hill, Holly, "Food Miles: Background and Marketing." National Center for Appropriate Technology ATTRA Sustainable Agriculture. 2008. www.attra.ncat.org/attra-pub/PDF/foodmiles.pdf.

Hocevar, John. "Circular Claims Fall Flat: Comprehensive US Survey of Plastic Recyclability." Greenpeace Inc. 2020. http://greenpeace.org/usa/plastic_recycling.

"Industrial Environmental Performance Metrics; Challenges and Opportunities." National Academies of Sciences Engineering Medicine. Chapter 7: The Pulp and Paper Industry. National Academies Press. 1999. https://www.nap.edu/read/9458/chapter/9.

Pirog, Richard S., and Andrew Benjamin. "Calculating Food Miles for a Multiple Ingredient Food Product." *Leopold Center Pubs and Papers* 147. 2005. http://lib.dr.iastate.edu/leopold_pubspapers/147.

Poore, J., and T. Nemecek. "Reducing Food's Environmental Impacts through Producers and Consumers." *Science* 360, no. 6392 (2018), 987–92.

Posen, I. Daniel, Paulina Jaramillo, Amy E. Landis, and W. Michael Griffin. "Greenhouse Gas Mitigation for U.S. Plastics Production: Energy First, Feedstocks Later." *Environmental Research Letters* 12 (March 2017). http://iopscience.iop.org/article/10.1088/1748-9326/aa60a7.

Ritchie, Hannah, and Max Roser. "CO_2 and Greenhouse Gas Emissions." Published online at OurWorldInData.org. 2020. https://ourworldindata.org/co2-and-other-greenhouse-gas-emissions.

Tita, Bob. "Recycling, Once Embraced by Businesses and Environmentalists, Now Under Siege." *Wall Street Journal*, May 13, 2018. https://www.wsj .com/articles/recycling-once-embraced-by-businesses-and-environmen talists-now-under-siege-1526209200?ns=prod/accounts-wsj.

United States Environmental Protection Agency (EPA). "Facts and Figures About Materials, Waste, and Recycling." 2018. https://www.epa.gov /facts-and-figures-about-materials-waste-and-recycling/containers -and-packaging-product-specific-data.

United States Environmental Protection Agency (EPA). "Final Air Toxics Standards for Clay Ceramics Manufacturing, Glass Manufacturing, and Secondary Nonferrous Metals Processing Area Sources: Fact Sheet." December 2007. https://www.epa.gov/sites/production/files/2016-04 /documents/2007_factsheet_areasources_clayceramics_glassmanufactur ing_secondarynonferrous_metals.pdf.

United States Environmental Protection Agency (EPA). "How Do I Recycle? Common Recyclables." 2021. https://www.epa.gov/recycle/how-do-i-re cycle-common-recyclables.

Weber, Christopher L. and H. Scott Matthews. "Food-Miles and the Relative Climate Impacts of Food Choices in the United States." *Environ. Sci. Technol.* 42, no. 10 (2008), 3508–13. DOI: https://doi.org/10.1021/es 702969f.

NEARLY ZERO-WASTE TOILETRIES

Erickson, Melinda L., Susan K. Langer, Jason L. Roth, and Sharon E. Kroening. "Contaminants of Emerging Concern in Ambient Groundwater in Urbanized Areas of Minnesota." US Geological Survey in partnership with Minnesota Pollution Control Agency. 2014. https://pubs.usgs.gov /sir/2014/5096/pdf/sir2014-5096.pdf.

Haereticus Environmental Laboratory. Protect Land + Sea Certification. 2018. http://haereticus-lab.org/protect-land-sea-certification-3.

United States Environmental Protection Agency (EPA). "R.E.D. Facts ***DEET***. Prevention Pesticides and Toxic Substances." 1998. (70508W). EPA-738-F-95-010. https://www3.epa.gov/pesticides/chem _search/reg_actions/reregistration/fs_PC-080301_1-Apr-98.pdf.

PET PROBLEMS

Blenderman, A., B. D. Taff, F. Schwartz, and B. Lawhon. "Dog Guardians' Perceptions and Behaviors Related to the Disposal of Pet Waste in City of Boulder Open Space and Mountain Parks." Final Report prepared for City of Boulder, Colorado, Open Space and Mountain Parks by Pennsylvania State University and the Leave No Trace Center for Outdoor

Ethics. 2018. https://lnt.org/wp-content/uploads/2018/10/2_2_18
_OSMP_Pet_Waste_Final_Report-1-201802051053.pdf.

"Boom or Bust: Will the COVID Pet Spike Last?" Pet Industry Distributors Association and American Pet Product Association. 2020. https://amer icanpetproducts.org/Uploads/MarketResearchandData/2021Stateofthe IndustryPresentationDeck.pdf.

Bosch, Guido, Esther Plantinga, and Wouter Hendriks. "Dietary Nutrient Profiles of Wild Wolves: Insights for Optimal Dog Nutrition?" *British Journal of Nutrition* 113. 10.1017/S0007114514002311. 2014. https:// www.researchgate.net/figure/Omnivorous-dog-traits-revisited-Dogs -are-classified-as-omnivores-based-on-traits-that_fig1_268743597.

Cinquepalmi, Vittoria, Rosa Monno, Luciana Fumarola, Gianpiero Ventrella, et al. "Environmental Contamination by Dog's Feces: A Public Health Problem?" *International Journal of Environmental Research and Public Health*, 10, no. 1 (2013), 72–84. doi: 10.3390/ijerph10010072.

Okin, G. S. "Environmental Impacts of Food Consumption by Dogs and Cats." *PLOS ONE* 12, no. 8 (2017). https://doi.org/10.1371/journal .pone.0181301.

Quinn, Adda. "Does Horse Manure Pose a Significant Risk to Human Health?" *EnviroHorse.* 2001. https://www.bayequest.com/static/pdf /manure.pdf.

Stevens, D., and A. Hussmann. "Wildlife Poop Versus Dog Poop: Explained." Leave No Trace. 2017. https://lnt.org/blog/wildlife-poop-versus-dog -poop-explained.

United States Department of Agriculture (USDA). Meat Price Spreads. 2021. https://www.ers.usda.gov/data-products/meat-price-spreads.

Winters, Ed (host). "Can Vegans Have Pets? The Pet Industry Explained." *In the Disclosure Podcast*, Episode 20, June 10, 2020. https://podcasts.apple .com/us/podcast/ep-20-can-vegans-have-pets-the-pet-industry-ex plained/id1451974673?i=1000477460136.

Bushcraft and Outdoor Minimalism

Sailer, Steve. "Name Game: 'Inuit' or 'Eskimo'?" 2002. https://www.upi.com /Odd_News/2002/06/20/Feature-Name-game-Inuit-or-Eskimo/431 91024597290/?u3L=1.

Leave It Better Than You Found It

Environment and Climate Change Canada (ECCC)'s National Inventory Report 1990–2018: *Greenhouse Gas Sources and Sinks in Canada*, submitted to the United Nations Framework Convention on Climate Change (UNFCCC) filed with the United Nations on April 14, 2020.

Geyer, Roland, Jenna R. Jambeck, and Kara L. Law. "Production, Use, and Fate of All Plastics Ever Made." *Science Advances* 3, no. 7 (July 19, 2017). DOI: 10.1126/sciadv.1700782.

Lau, Winnie W. Y., Yonathan Shiran, Richard M. Bailey, Ed Cook, et al. "Evaluating Scenarios Toward Zero Plastic Pollution." *Science* 69, no. 6510 (July 23, 2020), 1455–61. https://science.sciencemag.org/content /369/6510/1455.

Strategy for a Waste-Free Ontario: Building a Circular Economy. 2021. https://www.ontario.ca/page/strategy-waste-free-ontario-building -circular-economy.

United Nations Framework Convention on Climate Change (UNFCCC), filed with the United Nations on April 14, 2020.

About the Author

Meg Carney is a lifelong nature-lover and full-time outdoor and environmental writer. Her full portfolio can be found at megcarney .com. Along with personal writing projects, she is the senior editor of the CleanUp News, a news publication that focuses on environmental advocacy and educating consumers on the waste within the supply chain. Meg is well versed in outdoor activities like backpacking, rock climbing, trail running, and biking. If she isn't playing around in the dirt, you'll find her reading, writing, or enjoying a conversation with friends. Her combined passion for words and the environment has led her to lead a nomadic lifestyle with a career in writing and environmental advocacy.